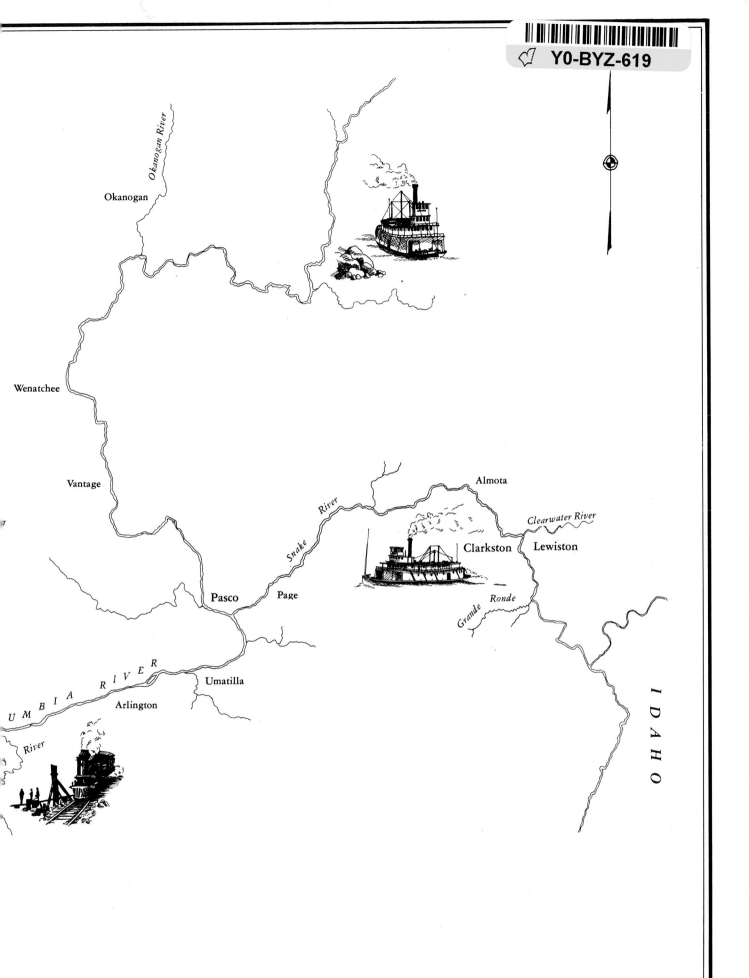

Okanogan River

Okanogan

Wenatchee

Vantage

Snake River

Almota

Clearwater River

Clarkston   Lewiston

Pasco   Page

Grande Ronde

C O L U M B I A   R I V E R

River

Umatilla

Arlington

I D A H O

Illustrations by James Bagley

This bronze chime whistle blew for many a landing, first on the Columbia River's famed "Hassalo," then on "Lewiston," one of the Union Pacific Railroad's Snake River boats. When "Lewiston" went north for the Alaska Railroad and retired as "Barry K," the chimer was returned to Portland and installed by Western Transportation Company on their stern-wheeler, "Claire." On her retirement, the whistle was placed on "Henderson" of the Shaver fleet. After almost sixty years of use, the bowl cracked beyond repair in a severe freeze.

BLOW FOR THE LANDING

A Hundred Years of Steam Navigation on the Waters of the West

FRITZ TIMMEN

4880 Lower Valley Road, Atglen, PA 19310 USA

Published by Schiffer Publishing Ltd.
4880 Lower Valley Road
Atglen, PA 19310
Phone: (610) 593-1777 FAX: (610) 593-2002
E-mail: Schifferbk@aol.com
Please write for a free catalog.
This book may be purchased from the publisher.
Please include $2.95 postage.
Try your bookstore first.

To
Sharon, My Wife, Who Understood.
And To
Kim, Peter, Kate and Carrie,
Who Someday Will.

WITH APPRECIATION

When it comes time to recall those who have given encouragement, assistance and sympathy during the fashioning of a book such as this, the author is beset by fears that he cannot adequately express thanks and, indeed, will not be able to properly acknowledge all those to whom thanks are due.

The principal coadjutors come readily to mind: Capt. Dennis Brown, Ed Culp, Thomas P. Guerin, Capt. Homer T. Shaver, W. B. Thayer, Herbert G. West, Victor C. West, and Wilfred Woods. The staff of the Oregon Historical Society deserves a special benison, as does Jim Bagley whose maps add meaning to the text.

For all I wish safe passage.

FRITZ TIMMEN
Lake Oswego, Oregon

April 28, 1972

TABLE OF CONTENTS

Page

LIST OF ILLUSTRATIONS

BLOW FOR THE LANDING

"J. N. Teal," Open River Transportation Company packet of 1907, below Cascade Locks.

BLOW FOR THE LANDING

No man who has seen the Columbia River will forget her.

If he has traveled the lower reaches, where relentless ocean tides push a hundred miles upstream against her thrust, he will remember the majestic, stately surge as she approaches the sea.

If he has stood on the shore at her union with the Snake, where in 1805 Lewis and Clark first saw her, he will remember how she rolled deeply, swiftly past as if gathering herself for the final three hundred miles of her journey.

Should he see her beginnings as the brawling outpouring of a mountain-rimmed lake, twelve hundred miles from where she meets the Pacific, he will know the promise of what she becomes — a power-laden giant, the nation's secondmost important commercial water artery.

From the beginning, men looked at the Columbia River as the most convenient passage through the Cascade and Coast ranges, a God-given natural highway with a built-in profit. So they turned their practical side out and began to build steamboats. Thus it was, a scant thirty years after Lewis and Clark put their canoes into its water, that the Columbia's fir clad hills gave back the hoot of a steam whistle.

But before that day came in 1836, there were only paddles and sails.

Earliest American contact with the Columbia was in 1792. On May eleventh of that year Captain Robert Gray became the first Yankee sailor to cross the entrance bar. His was less a voyage of exploration than of commerce. Existence of the river had been noted decades earlier by passing navigators who had not dared the shallow, tide-ripped entrance channel. Captain Gray was on a fur-trading mission and the hope that prime pelts could be bartered from the Columbia River Indians prompted this first crossing of the bar. When Gray returned to Boston his enthusiastic account and convincing profit sheet sent other commercial expeditions around the Horn and up the coast to the Pacific Northwest.

To secure the claim of the United States to the territory he had purchased from the Spaniards in 1803, President Thomas Jefferson dispatched the famed Lewis and Clark expedition of 1805/1806. Other overland parties quickly followed their path. Establishment of an American trading post at Astoria in 1811 by John Jacob Astor made obvious and inevitable the importance of the Columbia as a trade route.

Once Astor had pointed the way, competition for the lucrative fur business came rapidly. The North West

The steamer landing at Rooster Rock. Vista House, on Crown Point, commands a sweeping scene of the mouth of the Columbia Gorge, where the river leaves the Cascade Mountains and enters into tidewater.

Company, organized in Canada in 1775 for trapping and trading in the Eastern provinces, pushed westward across the Provinces in the 1780s and 1790s and down the Columbia River from its headwaters to the sea. During the War of 1812 the American post at Astoria was seized by the British, given over to the North West Company to operate, and named Fort George. The property was returned to United States owner-ship by international agreement in 1818.

Voyageurs and trappers of the North West Company depended on the Columbia as the fastest route to trading posts and forts in the interior. Getting there was a back-breaking combination of poling and paddling heavy canoes up the river, cordelling them through rapids and shallows, packing their cargo on men's backs around portages.

Hudson Bay voyageurs sailed, but more often laboriously poled, bateaux
laden with emigrants or Company furs.

The Hudson's Bay Company, successor to the North West Company, erected Fort Vancouver in 1824 near the junction of the Columbia and Willamette as western headquarters for the HBC's far flung empire. The Fort, a hundred miles above Astoria at the practical limit of deep water, became supply point for inland posts. From here annual brigades were dispatched to interior trapping grounds leaving Fort Vancouver in early spring and

At The Dalles, the covered wagon emigrant had a choice: he could struggle
afoot around Mount Hood or trust his luck by raft. Most took the water
route. They'd had enough of walking.

Before roads came, the river was the best way to travel. Steamboats carried settlers headed into new Columbia Basin lands.

ending the first leg of the journey at Fort Okanogan, some four hundred miles distant, in about sixty days. This was the upstream limit of navigation for bateaux, ungainly, scow-like craft, difficult to manage, but more commodious than canoes.

For trade and travel on the lower river and along the coast, Factor John McLoughlin about 1828 built the sailing vessels "Vancouver" and "Broughton."

In 1836 the "Beaver," first steamship on the Columbia, arrived at the fort from England. She had made the voyage under sail across the Atlantic and around the Horn. Her engines were connected after reaching Fort Vancouver. The "Beaver" served on the Columbia and later on British Columbia waters until she broke her back on a reef in 1886 near Vancouver, B.C.

After the "Beaver" left the river in the 1840s, steam navigation settled into the doldrums for about fifteen years. American settlers, who had been arriving in growing numbers since 1842, were too busy extracting Oregon from under British rule, building settlements, and getting their territorial government launched to think of commerce and trade on a wide scale. But by 1850 the population of Oregon and Washington territories had grown to the point where freer movement of people and goods was imperative. Esthetes arriving from the East demanded faster, more comfortable travel. Since early wagon roads and stage lines provided neither speed nor comfort travelers turned to the rivers.

In part, steamship building in its early stages became identified with municipal pride. Town promoters, filled with pecuniary zeal, stressed the importance of steamship service as a way of bringing trade to their communities.

Thus it happened that on a memorable July third in 1850 the jubilant populace of Astoria turned out to celebrate the launching of the river's first home-built steamboat. She was christened the "Columbia" and in appearance was a double-ended scow, without kitchen or cabin, or much else for the comfort of passengers. But she was the river's first steampowered craft built by Americans. Though her progress was faltering and her schedule uncertain, the Astorians pridefully loved every ungainly foot of her. The "Columbia" ran more or less regularly between Astoria and Oregon City and enjoyed unchallenged monopoly for some months.

But into the Willamette River at Milwaukie on the next Christmas Day slipped the "Lot Whitcomb," as elegant as the "Columbia" was not, with a handsome enclosed cabin, a parlor for the ladies, and a dining saloon. She was one hundred and sixty feet long, twenty-four feet wide, with a draft of five feet eight inches. By later standards the "Lot Whitcomb" was less than luxurious, but she was far more to be preferred than a stagecoach. She ran successfully until 1854 on the waters of the Columbia and Willamette, departing then to become the "Annie Abernethy" on the Sacramento River for the California Steam Navigation Company.

During 1851/52 a half dozen more competing craft were launched to accommodate an increasing Willamette Valley trade. Infrequent runs were made as far upstream as Eugene, about

Oregon's Chistmas present to itself in 1850 was "Lot Whitcomb," launched at Milwaukie to the oration of Governor Gaines and presented with an American flag by the mayor of Oregon City. A brass band, a fancy dress ball, and plenty of toasts marked the occasion. The festivities were marred only when a saluting cannon blew up, killing Captain Fred K. Morse.

one hundred twenty-five miles. Regular service was offered to Salem, Albany, and Corvallis.

The Mississippi River influence, which afflicted most of the early day steamers on Western waters, clearly shows in this painting of "Wallamet," built in 1853, for the middle Willamette run. No success there, she was lined over Willamette Falls and put in the Astoria trade as replacement for "Lot Whitcomb," which had recently been sold to California interests.

The Astoria-built "Columbia" extended her run to include the Portland-Cascades route, which it served until 1853, the first steamer on this reach of river. Finally faster, more commodious competitors forced her out of business and she ended her career ingloriously rotting on the river bank.

Steamboating on the middle Columbia River between the Cascades and

The Dalles was pioneered in 1851 by Daniel F. and Putnam Bradford. The year before, Francis A. Chenoweth had built a wooden track portage tramway a mile and a half long on the north side of the river around the Cascades. On this Chenoweth operated a mule-drawn car, but trade was almost non-existent and he soon sold out to the Bradford brothers. They, with J. O. Van

With scarcely room for another passenger or wagon, "Regulator" is loaded to the guards as she leaves the Cascades downbound for Portland.

Bergen, built the steamer "James P. Flint" at the lower end of the rapids. She was pulled above the Cascades on rollers, winched along by her own steam engine.

With Van Bergen as captain, the "Flint" operated above the Cascades, connecting with the schooner "Henry" below to establish regular service from Portland to The Dalles. In 1852, business fell off and the "Flint" was taken down through the rapids of the Cascades to run on the lower river. That September she struck a rock and sank near Cape Horn but the next year she was salvaged and repaired at Van-

couver. Renamed the "Fashion" and given the engines out of the "Columbia," she served honorably and well until she was dismantled in 1861.

Before long the scent of profits to be made in the freight and passenger trade reached the nostrils of other promoters who hastened to skim the cream off the emigrant trade. In 1853 Allan, McKinley & Company hauled the propeller boat "Allan" over the Cascades. The steam scow "Petonia" met the "Allan" at the Cascades to form a connecting link with Portland.

With control of the north bank portage tramway, the Bradfords

Steamboats consumed an average of four cords of wood an hour. Their hungry boilers provided gainful employment to hundreds of woodcutters. Barges, such as "Ella F," propelled by sail, carried cordwood to such timber-scarce upriver landings as The Dalles, from woodyards west of the Cascades. Much of Portland's Irvington district, once dense forest, was cut over to provide steamboat fuel.

The Oregon Portage Railroad was built of wood with strap iron rails. This 1867 scene was taken a half mile east of Bonneville. Bradford Island is on the left, Tooth Rock is on the far right, the mouth of Eagle Creek is in the middle distance. A shed for protection against falling rock straddles the track under Tooth Rock.

monopolized the middle river. By 1854 the "Allan" proved too small and too slow to handle increasing trade so the Bradfords, now joined by Captain Lawrence W. Coe, placed the side-wheel steamer "Mary" on the middle run to connect with the "Fashion," "Eagle," and "Belle" out of Portland. Shortly the "Hassaloe" was added to the middle river fleet with the "Mountain Buck" as connecting boat.

From all this competition erupted a rate war that dropped freight costs between Portland and The Dalles from near fifty dollars to thirty dollars per ton. Shippers rejoiced and business boomed for the boats.

In March 1856, the "Belle" played a dramatic role in diminishing one of the hazards of early-day navigation.

Local Indian tribes, egged on by the Yakima chief Kamiakan, were becoming increasingly restive at the encroachment of settlers. The redskins determined to teach the invaders a lesson and at the same time to wipe out the steamboat business. In an uprising at the Cascades they killed a number of whites but were not successful in burning the boats. A friendly Indian carried news of the attack to Fort Vancouver. Troops led by Lieutenant Philip H. Sheridan, who later distinguished himself in another, more bloody rebellion, raced to the scene on the "Belle," routed the Indians, and restored service on the river.

Accounts differ concerning construction of the first south bank opposition to the Bradfords. One report has it that W. R. Kilburn built in 1855, at the cost of one hundred fifty thousand dollars, a four-mile long wagon road around the Cascades on the Oregon shore and later sold it to Joseph S. Ruckel. Another story attributes construction of this route to Captain Van Bergen. The commonly accepted version is that Ruckel held a contract for furnishing supplies to troops maneuvering against Indians in the interior. The Bradfords refused to accept government vouchers in pay for hauling this plunder, and Ruckel was compelled to move the goods by mule-drawn wagons on a road hacked out around the Cascades on the Oregon side.

After the Indian trouble at the Cascades was put down, Ruckel, determined to settle his score with the Bradfords and make a profit to boot, associated himself with Harrison Olmstead, obtained a right-of-way and platted a permanent route on the south

Mules provided locomotion on the Oregon Portage Railroad for its first four years. One patiently poses on the bridge at Eagle Creek, headquarters and sawmill site of the portage company. It was cheaper to build trestles than to blast and clear rock, hence the extensive timber work.

shore. Incorporating themselves as the Oregon Portage Railroad, the two men hired J. W. Brazee to construct the road. Completed in the fall of 1858 it was of wooden rails faced with strap-iron. Horses and mules were the motive power for a string of flat cars.

Later, Ruckel and Olmstead obtained a steam locomotive which pulled twenty freight cars and one canopy-covered flat car as passenger equipment. This locomotive, now enshrined at Cascade Locks, was dubbed the "Oregon Pony".

Other operators soon appeared, notably a company including Captain J. C. Ainsworth and Jacob Kamm, which entered the fracas with the "Jennie Clark" in 1854 and the "Carrie Ladd" in 1858. The former bore the distinction of being the first stern-wheeler constructed in Oregon, all predecessor boats having been side-wheelers.

There was not enough business for the number of boats in the trade so the competitors engaged in the dangerous game of rate cutting. It soon became apparent this had to be stopped before all went broke. In 1859 a pool known as the Union Transportation Company was formed by owners of the "Carrie Ladd," "Jennie Clark," and "Express." Pending final organization, they chartered the "Mountain Buck" and "Senorita." This gave the combine control of the lower river fleet, and it was a simple matter to bring into line the "Mary" and "Hassaloe" on the middle river.

Meantime, transportation above

The "Oregon Pony," or its twin, sits in front of the shed.

The middle river boats "Dalles" (left), "Idaho," and "Iris" at The Dalles in a pre-1870 photo.

Celilo Falls was not going unattended. R. R. Thompson of The Dalles was owner of the only freight line on the upper river. His equipment was bateaux, mainly operated by Indians, who poled or rowed the craft or hoisted a sail when the wind was favorable. Thompson's terminal was at the mouth of the Deschutes River, twelve miles above The Dalles by the arduous portage road of Orlando Humason. Freight moved by Thompson went the one hundred and twenty miles from The Dalles to Wallula for one hundred dollars a ton.

In 1858 Thompson was joined by Captain L. W. Coe, erstwhile partner

The first "Hassalo" swings into The Dalles wharfboat past a loaded barge.

of the Bradfords, in an attempt to initiate steam transportation above Celilo Falls. They built the "Venture" at a shipyard near the Cascades on the middle river, intending to run her to Celilo and drag her above the falls. She left the bank under insufficient steam, was carried stern first over the Cascades, and hung up on a rock. Salvaged and repaired, the "Venture" was sent to the Fraser River. This misadventure prompted the partners to build their next boat above Celilo Falls.

The "Colonel Wright" was launched October 24, 1858, at the mouth of the Deschutes River, the first steamer to float above The Dalles. During the next spring, gold was discovered in Idaho's Clearwater River country and the "Wright" made several trips carrying supplies and prospectors to upriver points.

One of the most colorful of the river's early skippers was the "Wright's" master, Captain Leonard White. His youthful steamboating days had been spent on the Willamette River and his reputation led Thompson and Coe to engage him as pilot for their new vessel. That White was paid the then princely sum of five hundred dollars a month attests to the high esteem afforded him.

Captain White made three trips weekly between Celilo portage and Fort Walla Walla carrying capacity loads of freight and passengers. He also took the "Wright" on her historic first trip up the Snake, nearly coming to grief at the mouth of the Palouse River. The "Wright" struck a submerged snag, was holed, and almost sank before Captain White could beach her. After

repairs were made, the "Wright" resumed her Celilo-Wallula chores.

Later, in high water, Captain White took his boat to Lewiston, becoming the first man to make a landing there.

A few adventuresome skippers, Len White included, believed the Snake could be navigated above Lewiston. In 1862 White built a new boat expressly for this purpose and successfully pushed it as far upstream as Pittsburgh Landing, seventy-seven miles from Lewiston.

Other intrepid steamboatmen successfully operated on the Snake but not without difficulty. There still is visible evidence in the form of a huge ringbolt sunk in a granite boulder at Mountain Sheep Rapids. This treacherous stretch of water, a short distance above the mouth of the Salmon River, proved too much for stern-wheelers to navigate without help.

Hanging at the foot of the rapids, engines racing to hold her against the current, the boat would wait while the crew dragged a stout manila line along the shore and attached it to the ringbolt above the rapids. Then the foredeck capstan would slowly wind in the rope, dragging the boat through the rapids into slower water above. It was another mile from Mountain Sheep Rapids to Eureka Bar, the practical head of navigation for prospectors working gravel bars on the Snake, the Imnaha, and other tributaries.

Under command of Captain Thomas Stump the "Colonel Wright" in the spring of 1865 attempted to fight her way through Hells Canyon of the Snake to Farewell Bend. But she made only about one hundred miles of the dis-

tance. The upriver trip took eight days;
she came roaring down to Lewiston in
five hours. The gallant "Wright" was
worn out by her effort. She was broken
up in August, 1865, and her engines
were placed in the "Mary Moody" on
Lake Pend d'Oreille.

Thompson and Coe were made
wealthy by the revenues returned from
the "Wright." The partners supplemented her with the "Tenino," a
larger, more powerful craft built at
Celilo Falls in 1860. This new addition
proved even more profitable. On a
single trip in May, 1862, her purser
turned in ten thousand, nine hundred

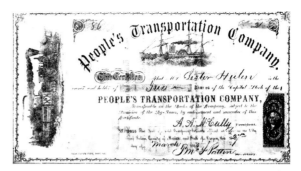

It is not recorded how much Lester Hulen paid for
his two shares of People's Transportation Company
stock, but he joined a host of stockholders scattered
along the Willamette from Eugene to Portland.

The Northern Pacific's insignia dominates the pilot house of "J. M. Hannaford," the big freight boat built
at Potlatch, Idaho, in 1899 for Snake River service. Her twin stacks evoke memories of the Mississippi.

and forty five dollars for passenger fares and enough additional from freight, meals, and berths to swell the total to more than eighteen thousand dollars.

During the summer of 1862 lively opposition began to develop on the river. D. S. Baker, A. P. Ankeny, H. W. Corbett, William Gates, and Captain Harry Baughman formed a company and built the "Spray" to run on the upper Columbia and Snake. She made fourteen trips to Lewiston her first season and paid for herself three times over in the first five months of operation.

The People's Transportation Company put a competing line of steamboats on the river that year. Incorporators of this line included Davis and Asa McCully, J. W. Cochrane, E. W. Baughman, Joseph Kellogg, George Jerome, D. W. Burnside, S. T. Church, and E. N. Cooke.

Most of these ventures were designed to capture business from the Oregon Steam Navigation Company, emerging from its 1860 incorporation as the many-tentacled monopoly of river transportation. The O. S. N. was the direct descendant of the Union Transportation Company of 1859.

Papers incorporating the Oregon Steam Navigation Company were filed at Vancouver, Washington, December 29, 1860. The largest stockholders were D. F. Bradford, R. R. Thompson, Harrison Olmstead, Jacob Kamm, J. C. Ainsworth, and L. W. Coe. Incorporation under Oregon laws was effected at Portland, October 18, 1862, with capital of two million dollars.

Shortly, by merger or purchase, the O.S.N. acquired most of the boats on the Columbia and Snake River. Between Portland and the Cascades it operated the "Senorita," "Fashion," "Julia," "Belle," "Mountain Buck," and "Carrie Ladd." Above the Cascades to the Celilo portage ran the "Mary," "Hassaloe," "Wasco," and "Idaho." The "Tenino" and the "Colonel Wright" were the upper river connecting boats. Since control of the portage facilities meant domination of river commerce, the O.S.N. bought not only the Olmstead south bank road and the Bradford holdings at the Cascades, but also purchased the portage around Celilo Falls which had been build by Orlando Humason.

The mule-drawn wooden tramway on the north bank at the Cascades was replaced in 1863 with steel rails and locomotives, and the stage was set for the tremendous developments which followed under the domination of the O.S.N., Oregon's first monopoly.

A first class rail line, thirteen miles long, was built from The Dalles around Celilo Falls and opened for use on April 23, 1863. This road, which cost one million dollars to construct, operated until a railroad was built from The Dalles to Wallula fifteen years later.

With Columbia River traffic under its control, the O.S.N. levied passenger and freight charges at what the traffic would bear. Prices fluctuated depending upon the pressure of competition from small lines which periodically attempted to oppose the company.

Typical freight charges per ton ran:

Portland to The Dalles (121 miles) $15.00
Portland to Umatilla (217 miles) 45.00
Portland to Wallula (240 miles) 50.00
Portland to Lewiston (401 miles) 90.00

Three "Hassalos" (and one "Hassaloe") served the Columbia. The last, launched in 1899, could turn up twenty-six miles an hour.

All freight costs were figured by measurement, forty cubic feet equalling one ton. A Lewiston merchant in 1862 received a crated shipment of miner's shovels that measured a cubic ton and held ninety shovels. At a freight cost of ninety dollars a ton, tariff on each shovel was one dollar.

Perhaps not entirely apocryphal is the story of an O.S.N. agent at The Dalles who was taking measurements on a small mounted cannon, part of an

Army shipment. A couple of lounging soldiers watched with interest as the clerk measured the weapon several ways and pencilled out his calculations. Sensing perplexity, a soldier asked what the problem was. The clerk replied that he couldn't get his figures to come out right. "That's easy," the soldier said. He led up a pair of harnessed mules and hitched them to the cannon. "Try it now," he suggested.

The beaming clerk marked off the length of the gun and the span of mules, scaled off the height from ground to ear tips and announced that now his measurements were correct.

During the peak of gold rush travel, passenger fares were twenty three dollars from Portland to Wallula. Passage from Portland to The Dalles was eight dollars, with an additional levy for portage at the Cascades, plus seventy-five

Courtesy Oregon Historical Society

Captain John Anderson of "Hassalo" assumed a properly dignified mien as he posed with his crew. At his right is his Chief Engineer, whose name is forgotten, Pilot Andy Anderson is at the Captain's left. Standing at left is Harold Bain, Freight Clerk, with Mate Chester Turner next, sided by Purser Victor Dalgdeish. The Steward is also unidentified.

"Monarch" assists a distressed lumber schooner, decks almost awash and down by the stern.

cents for meals. From the Deschutes to Wallula the fare was fifteen dollars, with meals free. Patronage at the bar was extra. Transportation for animals from Portland to The Dalles was five dollars.

An advertisement published by the Walla Walla Statesman on May 17, 1862, listed the following accommodations:

FOR NEZ PERCE MINES
The Oregon Steam Navigation Company's
steamers will run on the
Columbia River as follows:
The Steamer "Julia"
Wolf . . . . .Commander
Will leave Portland every Monday,
Wednesday and Friday at 6 P. M.
connecting with
The Steamer
"Idaho"
MacNulty . . . . .Commander
At the Cascades for The Dalles
City, arriving same day.
New Steamer "Tenino"
White . . . . .Commander
Will leave Deschutes for Wallula
every Tuesday; returning, leaves
Wallula each Thursday at 6 A.M.

When rival ventures arose the O.S.N.

simply dropped rates until the squeeze forced the upstarts off the river. In 1862 The People's Transportation Company was formed by most of the river men not already involved with the O.S.N. This new corporation waged a rate war so successfully that the O.S.N. offered its rival a bonus of ten thousand dollars a year to confine its activities to the Willamette. The agreement was observed for ten years, when The People's Company sold out to railroad builder Ben Holladay. Holladay subsequently suffered financial reverses and sold his holdings to the O.S.N., completing the circle begun more than a decade earlier.

Increasing travel prompted the O.S.N. to extend its fleet, and in 1863 the "Webfoot" and "Nez Perce Chief" went on the upriver run with the "Oneonta" added to the middle river flotilla. A year later the "Owyhee" and "Yakima" were built at Celilo.

To improve service between Portland and upriver points, the side-wheel steamer, "New World," was brought out from the East. She made the trip the hard way, around South America and up the coast to California. After a brief stop-off at the Sacramento River, she served on the Columbia until transferring to Puget Sound in 1868.

Light freight and passengers continued to be the biggest revenue source. The rush of miners continued. On one arrival in Portland from California the coastwise steamship, "Brother Jonathan," landed a thousand seekers, all in haste to reach the diggings regardless of cost. The "Nez Perce Chief," on one down trip from Lewiston during the height of the rush, hauled three hundred and eighty two thousand dol-

She began as a towboat, but "Hattie Belle" (1892) shortly graduated to the Cascades freight-passenger route. Here she meets the train at Moffitt's Landing.

lars worth of gold dust and bars securely locked in the captain's safe.

One of the queens of the steamboat fleet was the handsome "Yakima," which held the speed record of forty-one hours, thirty-five minutes from

When the east wind came howling down the Columbia Gorge and pack ice began building, there wasn't much a wooden-hulled steamboat could do but tie up and wait it out. It was six weeks before "Sarah Dixon" and "Regulator" got out of Cascade Locks in the winter of 1909.

"Joseph Kellogg," "Capital City," and steam tug "Maja" wait out the break-up in the lee of Stanley Rock in 1907.

Celilo portage to Lewiston. The distance covered was two hundred and sixty miles, much of it through rapids that funneled the full force of the Columbia and Snake rivers into rocky chutes, often at speeds of fifteen miles an hour.

Columbia River steamboats were designed and built specifically for the purpose of coping with just such conditions. There hulls were long and narrow, their draft slight. But some managed to carry as many as five hundred passengers, crowded into every available inch of space, and to haul as much as five hundred tons of freight to boot. When the Columbia and Snake reached low water stages the freight haul was reduced, but operations seldom completely ceased except during severest icing conditions in winter, or at the peak of summer freshets.

Two favorite refuges from threatening ice packs were at Cold Springs Harbor, on the Columbia River a short distance above Umatilla, and at Ice Harbor on the Snake, about ten miles above its mouth. To these protected shelters the captains ran when ice jams made travel impossible during the spring breakup. Ice Harbor is gone now, drowned in the backwaters of Lake Sacajawea, but it is possible to make out the perimeters of the protecting bay.

Early in the spring of 1862 the "Colonel Wright" lay at the wharf at Fort Walla Walla, near the mouth of the Walla Walla River. She had reached there on her way up to Lewiston, burdened with all the plunder necessary to build and equip a first-class saloon, gambling hall, and honky-tonk. The passenger list was liberally sprinkled with gamblers, bartenders, and an attractive collection of dance-hall hostesses and female vaudeville entertainers.

Ice was still flowing too heavily in the Snake to permit safe passage, and Captain Len White prudently decided to wait a few days. The word spread among the woman-hungry bachelors on nearby ranches that the "Wright's" most important cargo wore perfume.

A pair of horseless carriages share deck space with a farm wagon aboard "J. N. Teal" in the lower lock at the Cascades. The team probably munches oats on the freight deck, blissfully unaware that the automobile will spell not only its doom but that of the steamboat as well.

The boat was besieged. In panic, Captain White cast off for the more isolated shelter of Ice Harbor. His strategy failed. By canoe, raft, and rowboat, amorous single males for miles around sought out the steamer. By the time the troupe was delivered at Lewiston, its manager had to send back to Portland for additional female personnel. But ranch life in Franklin, Whitman, and Walla Walla counties was a lot less lonely from then on.

Steamers seldom made the Snake River run to Lewiston when the gauge there read less than three feet. At that stage the water was too shallow to allow pay loads. However, Captain Arthur Riggs once took the "J. N. Teal" with fifty tons of freight to Lewiston when the gauge registered only one and seven tenths feet. Which is not much more depth of water than is required to take a bath.

For good reason, stern-wheel steamers were considered the most practical craft for the shallow, open-river conditions found on the Columbia and Snake. With the engines then available more power could be developed by a paddle wheel than by a propeller. Shallow rapids allowed little room under the hull for propellers of suitable size. Paddle wheels needed very little "dip," or submergence, in proportion to hull draft.

Too, the stern-wheeler proved more maneuverable, particularly in backing. Ability to back and drift, with enough rudder power to swing the stern from port to starboard with facility, was essential in swift water navigation. A stern-wheeler could more quickly overcome the inertia of a loaded boat than could one driven by a screw pro-

peller. This was important in descending swift, tortuous channels when quick changes, of course, could only be made by prompt reversing and flanking.

There was another point in favor of stern-wheelers: should the vessel lose a few wheel buckets on a rock she could still proceed, though at reduced speed, until she could tie up at the bank. The crew then could make repairs without troubling to haul the craft out of the water.

Of necessity, early steamboat hulls were made of wood, preferred by captains and owners even after iron hull construction became possible. Initial cost and upkeep of wood hulls were less. The boats kept striking submerged rocks and grounding on gravel bars, and the heavy planking of wood hulls would slide by with little damage other than scarring. If the jolt was severe and a plank was shattered, the result was only fast seepage instead of an inrush of water.

Standard procedure for repairing a wooden hull was to spike a soft patch over the damaged section until permanent repairs could be made. Some Snake River skippers operated during the busy season with as many as a hundred soft patches on the hull varying from four to sixty feet long. Replacing planks or frames was a simple matter compared with removing and replacing entire sections of steel plating.

Portland by the mid-1860s was well on its way to becoming a thriving port. Its merchants were shaking off the domination of San Francisco ownership which had reduced many business

"Regulator" poses with Beacon Rock in the background in this 1899 winter scene.

houses along Front Street to branch operations. *The Daily Portland Herald* took up the cry, urging citizens to establish foreign commerce and an independent trade for Oregon. Its editors pointed out that flour milled at Salem was marketed as "California Flour." San Francisco commission merchants, reshipping goods from the east which had been unloaded at San Francisco with Portland as final destination, were taking nearly one million, two hundred thousand dollars a year in commissions plus another four hundred thousand in freight charges off the top. "Why do we consent to being a mere dependency?" the editorialists cried.

Stirred by such chauvinism, private Portland money was raised to start independent shipping lines between the Columbia River and California, and, soon, to Hawaii, China, Australia, and Europe.

A variety of Oregon products began to find new markets. Boxed apples, barrelled salt salmon, butter, flour, eggs, gunnies of bacon, livestock, potatoes, and lumber appeared on bills of lading. But by far the most significant export until 1870 was listed as "treasure." This was gold dust and ingots pouring out of Idaho and Montana mines to the San Francisco mint.

In 1865, Portland's exports amounted to $7,606,524, gold the greatest part of it. In 1867 the total was $6,463,793 with about four million dollars documented as treasure.

As settlers increased in eastern Oregon and Washington they began to demand transportation to market for their grain. For a long time the Oregon Steam Navigation Company refused to haul such low-grade freight. But as gold veins petered out and as shack towns and tent cities of the miners dwindled to ghosts, grain cargoes looked more attractive. It was up to the farmer to deliver his sacked grain to the river bank where steamboats could reach it. After he paid for the land haul to the river and for steamer freight and portages, return to the grower was meager. Wheat from Walla Walla and points

"Harvest Queen" nudges a square rigger, full and by, into the channel at Portland for the one hundred mile tow to the Columbia River bar.

upstream was handled six times before it finally landed at the docks at Portland.

Although freight rates on the river had standardized at twenty dollars a ton, the O.S.N. Company, in a later effort to attract traffic, made a rate of seven dollars and fifty cents a ton on flour and wheat from Wallula to Portland. But when the first downriver shipment arrived in Portland the *Oregonian* commented, "It was like shipping coals to New Castle, and the farmers of the Willamette Valley need not worry as Walla Walla flour can never affect their market."

Then, as if to prove it hadn't yet caught up with the times, the O.S.N. advanced the freight rate on flour shortly after the service was begun. The Walla Walla *Statesman* complained; "At a time when the rates of transportation are being lowered, and low freight rates are the order of the day, it will surprise the public to learn that the O.S.N. Company had advanced the rate on flour shipped from Wallula to The Dalles, from seven dollars and fifty cents to seventeen dollars and fifty cents a ton. It is only a few weeks since the business of shipping produce from this place was fairly inaugurated, and

A railroad boat, "Almota" (1876) was built by the O.S.N. and spent most of her career on the Snake. She had great cargo capacity and was a big money earner.

now before the experiment can fairly be said to have had a trial, the O.S.N. Company, by means of exorbitant tariff, endeavors to stifle the movement in its infancy."

The company paid attention to the protest and dropped its down-bound rates. Flour shipped to Portland from April 19 to June 2, 1867, came to four thousand, seven hundred and thirty-five barrels. The cost was six dollars a ton.

Increasing commerce on the river brought the need for larger boats, but to accommodate them shallow channels first had to be deepened. The O.S.N. appealed to the federal government for help, and in 1867 the Corps of Engineers was ordered to make a survey of the Columbia from Celilo Falls to the mouth of the Snake River. Lieutenant W. H. Hover commanded the expedition. Pilot of the survey boat was W. P. Gray. Later he related: "I was engaged as captain under the title of assistant engineer to navigate the sailing schooner that carried the party up and down the river. It took us two seasons of low water to complete the survey and soundings of the rapids.

"During the next few years the rapids at John Day, Squally Hook, Owyhee, Devil's Bend, Umatilla, and Homly on the Columbia, and Five Mile, Fishhook, Pine Tree, Monumental, Palouse and Texas on the Snake were improved at a cost of several hundred thousands of dollars, supplemented by a considerable amount by the steamboat company in removing several dangerous rocks that the government engineers could not find, but some of the pilots found to the damage of their boats."

"Lytton," built at Revelstoke, B.C., in 1890, ran for the Columbia & Kootenai Steam Navigation Company between Robson and Little Dalles until 1903. "Lytton" was one of a half dozen boats that served the rich mining districts along border lakes and on connecting rivers.

"Lewiston" running the daily routine of a Pacific Northwest utility boat: nose to the bank long enough to muscle the freight aboard and throw off the mail, possibly pick up a couple of paying passengers, then on to the next mud landing.

With improved navigating conditions, steamboats hauled larger payloads. Shortly, warehouses sprang up at several river points between Pasco and Lewiston. At one time there were forty-seven landings on this one

"Spokane" loads sacked wheat at a river landing.

hundred and forty mile stretch of river, one about every three miles.

For some distance downstream from Lewiston, the Snake flows between steep canyon walls. The prime wheat-producing land is on high benches overlooking the river. To solve the problem of getting grain to the river landings, Major Sewell Truax of Walla Walla developed in 1879 a grain chute that was the epitome of ingenuity.

From the major's wheat fields on the bluffs to the river bank below was built a four-inch by four-inch wooden pipe three thousand, two hundred feet long. To slow down the bulk grain and to

prevent friction from burning it during the pell-mell descent, the chute was fitted at one hundred foot intervals with baffle plates. Wind currents, kicked up by the flowing grain, carried dust and smut out through vents installed above each baffle. When it reached the warehouse at the bottom of the bluff, the wheat was sacked, and loaded onto steamers.

The ingenious Major Truax gained further advantage from his delivery system by dumping the grain into a hopper so it fell on an overshot wheel as it entered the chute. Thus grain became the motive power for agitating a cleaning screen, or any other machinery the inventive major cared to attach to his wheel.

Within a couple of years five such chutes, two owned by Truax, were at work along the Snake. One was at Kelley's Bar, some nine miles below Alpowa. The Paine brothers of Walla Walla built one a half-mile long, with a fall of eighteen hundred feet, about a mile downstream from Hemingway's Landing, and S. Galbreath located his chute across the Snake from Wawawai.

Shortly after 1900 a tramway was con-

structed in the Mayview region to haul sacked wheat from the high bench to the river landing. Two cars served the tramway, the downbound load bringing the empty car to the top.

By 1878 seven more big steamers had been added to the O.S.N. fleet: the "Harvest Queen," "John Gates," "Spokane," and "Annie Faxon," built at Celilo; the "Mountain Queen" and "R. R. Thompson," built at The Dalles; the "Wide West," built at Portland.

The "Harvest Queen" was a veritable floating palace, the finest and fas-

"Columbia" loading grain at Chelan Falls landing, 1905. This photo shows the grain chutes used to get the product to the river.

Youngsters delighted in riding the wave as the second "Harvest Queen" glided by.

test steamboat on the upper river. She was two hundred feet long with a thirty-seven foot beam and seven and one half foot depth of hold. She could carry five hundred tons of cargo. Command of the "Queen" was given to twenty-three year old Captain James W. Troup. Some years later, when she left the upper river run, Captain Troup took her full steam ahead over the falls at Celilo in one of the river's more memorable passages.

Construction of these vessels proved to be the last great spurt of the Oregon Steam Navigation Company. After nineteen years of highly profitable operation its stock and assets were sold in June, 1879. The purchasers were Henry Villard and ten partners who put six million dollars on the line. The shrewd businessmen who had built the O.S.N. and found it profitable retired from the transportation industry. Most of them invested in other enterprises

..THE..

Oregon Railroad and Navigation Co.'s

NEW STEAMER

"Hassalo"

Now Carrying the World's Record as the Fastest Stern-Wheel Steamboat.

... IS NOW PLYING BETWEEN . .

PORTLAND AND ASTORIA.

A poster advertising the famous O. R. & N. steamer "Hassalo."

and some of Portland's present-day family fortunes trace their beginning back to the days of the O.S.N.

Oregon's first monopoly passed out of existence, only to be replaced by another.

The emerging combine was the Oregon Railroad & Navigation Company. In the transaction, the O. R. & N. had acquired nearly every worthwhile stern-wheeler on the Columbia. The floating equipment that changed hands included the "Wide West," "Emma Hayward," "S. G. Reed," "Fannie Patton," "S. T. Church," "McMinnville," "Ocklahama," "E. N. Cook," "Governor Grover," "Alice," "Bonita," "Dixie Thompson," "Wel-

come," "R. R. Thompson," "Mountain Queen," "Idaho," "Annie Faxon," "John Gates," "Harvest Queen," "Spokane," "New Tenino," "Almota," "Willamette Chief," "Orient," "Occident," "Bonanza," "Champion," and "D. S. Baker."

The O. R. & N. Company used these boats and the portages of its predecessor to advantage in the construction of a rail line between Celilo and Wallula. The traditional Golden Spike was driven in April, 1881, and in October of the next year the link connecting Portland with The Dalles and the Inland Empire was completed at Multnomah Falls.

In 1881 opposition to the O. R. & N. began to develop on the lower and middle rivers. Captain U. B. Scott and his associates, L. B. Seely and E. W. Creighton, built the fast propeller boat, "Fleetwood," for the Cascades route.

Courtesy Oregon Historical Society

The big O. R. & N. boat, "Annie Faxon."

One of the finer passenger boats on the Portland-Cascades run was "Charles R. Spencer." After that trade was doomed by the automobile, she was rebuilt as "Monarch," shown here.

Under signs announcing schedule and fares, the Astoria boats, "Undine" and "Lurline," wait at the O. W. R. & N. two-level dock at the foot of Ash Street.

The propeller "Gold Dust," constructed for Captain E. W. Spencer in 1880 and originally used on the Portland-Vancouver route, was hauled over the Cascades to compete with O. R. & N. boats on the middle river. Because of stiff rate competition, passengers soon were enjoying a fifty cent fare from Portland to The Dalles.

The O. R. & N. Company figured prominently in an 1882 crime described by one contemporary chronicler as a "horrible and mysterious affair." This was the murder and robbery of E. H. Cummins, agent for the company at New York Bar on the Snake River in Columbia County, Washington.

With thorough attention to detail the account states: "On the twenty-sixth of July, 1882, his dead body was found on the bed in which he slept, dressed only in shirt and drawers, with a heavy quilt thrown over it and a doubled quilt across his feet. There was one bullet wound in the hand, one in the right hip, one in the left shoulder, one in the back, and two in the back of the head; also an axe wound on top of the head, one across the mouth and one over the eye; the throat had been cut with a knife severing the juglar[sic] and windpipe. Seven bullets and bullet holes were found in the cabin, making a probable total of thirteen shots fired at the man before the axe and knife were used. About one thousand dollars of the money of the O. R. & N. Company in possession of the deceased, were secured by the murderers. Several arrests have been made, but with no direct and satisfactory testimony to rely upon. The short time that has elapsed since the bloody deed was committed, gives the citizens hope that the perpetrators may be discovered and punished."

The Columbia County sheriff and his posse diligently but fruitlessly pursued clues and false leads. Railroad detectives brought in by the O. R. & N. tracked down the culprits, Canada Owensby, J. H. McPherson, and Ezra Snodderly. Their trial, held at Dayton, Washington, in December, 1882, resulted in conviction. McPherson's lawyers appealed, and the territorial supreme court ruled a retrial should be held in another locality. This piqued the local vigilante group, who took McPherson forcibly from the Dayton jail and hanged him from a waiting scaffold in the yard.

Snodderly's appeal failed, and he was legally hanged. But Canada Owensby, who had been moved to Walla Walla for safekeeping after the McPherson lynching, escaped and fled into the Blue Mountains. He was tracked down, near exhaustion from hunger and bitter weather, and returned to confinement. The ordeal proved too much, and within a few weeks he was dead of pneumonia and other complications.

The O. R. & N. Company found the middle river boat line an expensive service to operate, with two portages to maintain and two transfers of freight at each portage. It simply was sound business to withdraw the boats from service and dispose of them. This the company did as soon as possible, bringing the fleet down to Portland from the upper and middle river.

Captain Troup had taken the

After twenty years as a connecting boat on the middle Cascades run, "Idaho" (1860) was sent to Puget Sound. She operated on several trans-Sound runs, ending as a mission and hospital on Seattle's waterfront.

"Harvest Queen" over Celilo Falls into the middle river in 1881. She served on this reach until 1890, when the same pilot took her over the Cascades to the lower river. Captain Troup also brought the "D. S. Baker" over Celilo Falls in 1888. In 1893 he moved her down through the Cascades to Portland.

In the meantime, work was plodding forward on construction of a canal around the Cascades. As early as 1875, in response to numerous requests, the Corps of Engineers had surveyed the rapids and recommended a canal be built around the upper section. Congress appropriated ninety thousand dollars to get work started. When it was discovered this amount was just a beginning, the Federal purse strings tightened. But enough funds were added annually to keep hopes up and crews digging for almost the next decade.

When the south bank railroad was completed by the O. R. & N. in 1883, even this small amount of interest in a canal dwindled. A further blow was struck when the company began moving its middle river fleet below the Cascades. This left shippers no choice but to use the railroad which adjusted its prices upwards. The hue and cry raised by Central Oregon and Washington wheat men at this maneuver reverberated through the halls of Congress. In 1893 the substantial sum of $1,239,653 was appropriated and completion of the Cascades canal and locks was assured.

Total cost ran to nearly eight million dollars. The locks were in two steps: the lower chamber was four hundred and ninety feet long, the upper chamber four hundred and two feet.

The second "Harvest Queen" making fast at St. Helens.

The trim little "Manzanillo," shown at Clatskanie in 1895, was built in 1881 by Captain Charles Bureau, and when acquired by the Shaver family in 1884, became the nucleus of a family business that yet is active.

Both were ninety feet wide. Lift on the lower was twenty-four feet and on the upper eighteen feet.

Rejoicing at the completion was great. At the dedication exercises in November, 1896, were boats of the Shaver Transportation Company, the O. R. & N., and of The Dalles, Portland & Astoria Navigation Company, the "Regulator Line." Through the locks went the Shaver's "Sarah Dixon," four years old and already proven a fast packet. Then the "Dalles City" and the "Regulator," owned by the D. P. & A. N., made the passage, flags flying and passengers waving and cheering.

An understanding had been reached with Captain James W. Shaver that the "Regulator" would be the first boat at The Dalles. To Captain George M.

Shaver, at the wheel of the "Sarah Dixon," this was unthinkable. With the connivance of some of the ladies on board, Captain James was lured into a cabin to join the celebration and mirth around the piano. While Captain James was thus diverted, Captain George instructed the chief engineer to fire up the boilers with pitchwood. The safety valve was screwed down, the "Regulator" was left astern, and the "Sarah Dixon" triumphantly pulled into The Dalles to the huzzahs of the citizens half an hour ahead of the fuming master of the rival boat.

Captain James was irate that he had been hoodwinked, but he subsided when the owners of the D. P. & A. N. offered the Shaver firm two hundred and fifty dollars a month to stay off the

From the *Pacific Monthly*, February, 1904.

middle river and leave the pickings to its steamboats.

A short time later Shaver Transportation Company was made the same offer by the O. R. & N. to quit competing with the "T. J. Potter" on the Portland-Astoria run. The accommodating Shavers put the "Sarah Dixon" and others of their fleet on the Clatskanie route and similar shortline passenger and freight hauls for a number of years.

But completion of the Cascade locks failed to produce the traffic volume that years before had made fortunes for owners of the Oregon Steam Navigation Company. Although passenger business held up, promised shipper support fell away, and opening of the North Bank Railway in 1905 provided owners of the Regulator Line an opportunity to unload. Ownership passed to the hands of James J. Hill, controlling genius of the Great Northern, Northern Pacific, and Spokane, Portland & Seattle Railway (the North Bank Line).

Steamer "Regulator" at Rooster Rock.

"State of Washington" in the lower lock at the Cascades.

Higher up on the Columbia River, Entiat Rapids was a favorite spot for snapping a steamboat's portrait. "Selkirk" obliges with the help of a scenic background.

The railroad company's plans for operation of its steamboat fleet jointly with its rail line ended when the Panama Canal Act in 1912 made it illegal for a railroad to own and control a competing boat line. The fleet was sold in 1915.

The last great barrier to free and open navigation of the Columbia River from its mouth to the interior lay at Celilo Falls. For more than eight miles the river churned and boiled through one series of impassable rapids after another. The only passage around this obstacle was by portage. In 1858, the first wagon road, nineteen miles long, was constructed. By 1863, this had been replaced by the Oregon Steam Navigation Company's thirteen mile portage railroad. This line, costing six hundred and fifty thousand dollars to construct, operated until 1882 when it became a link in Henry Villard's south bank rail line that eventually became the Union Pacific.

But portages were an unsatisfactory solution. Farmers and merchants wanted through boat service. Delays and costs of double handling at the portages were unacceptable. Cries for an

"City of Ellensburgh," first steamboat in the Wenatchee area, works her way through Entiat Rapids. She was built at Pasco in 1888 by Ellensburg interests.

"Umatilla," Corps of Engineers dredge, passes through a rock cut in Celilo Canal during late construction phases.

open river were raised the length of the Columbia.

In answer to the problem, the Corps of Engineers proposed an elaborate railway that would hydraulically hoist steamboats from the river at the foot of Five Mile Rapids and transport them eight miles to the head of Celilo Falls. To this end between August, 1894, and June, 1896, Congress appropriated two hundred and fifty thousand dollars for planning and right-of-way purchase. Work commenced in 1898, and some thirty thousand dollars had been spent by the end of the 1900 fiscal year.

By then, folly of the scheme had become clear. Congress ordered all work halted while a study was made on the feasibility and cost of a canal. Back to the drawing board went the Corps. In reality, they had been there since 1874, when improvements to this reach of river first came under federal scrutiny. An 1879 survey recommended a canal on the Washington shore at an estimated cost of seven million six hundred thousand dollars. No action was taken. In 1888, a second canal plan was proposed, this time on the Oregon shore, at a cost of about three million seven hundred thousand dollars. Again, the idea was shelved.

"Tahoma" served any community that provided enough water to float in.

Affairs stagnated until 1892 when a board of Army Engineers proposed a two-pronged approach — a portage road first and a canal at a later date. It was from this report that the abortive boat-railroad idea stemmed.

In designing a canal and lock system to circumvent this most tortuous reach of the Columbia River, the Corps of Engineers faced a formidable task. On the upriver end of this caldron was Celilo Falls, a twenty foot drop over a ledge of basalt. Next came Tenmile Rapids, a half-mile of boiling foam. Fivemile Rapids stretched for one and one-half miles, compressing the whole flow of the Columbia between sheer rock walls less than three hundred feet apart. Below were Big Eddy and Threemile Rapids and then calm waters just above the town of The Dalles.

By 1900 the new plan was ready. It called for two locks and a three thousand foot canal around Celilo Falls, a thirty-three foot lift lock, a nine thousand foot canal around Fivemile Rapids, with a submerged dam at the head of these rapids, and the improvement of navigation at Threemile Rapids. The whole project was to cost four million dollars.

Congress approved the project on June 13, 1902. It authorized the remaining unexpended funds from the portage railroad scheme to get work underway. In May, 1903, a hearing at Portland modified the plans to provide for a continuous canal with four locks from Big Eddy to the head of Celilo Falls. The Secretary of the Army stamped his approval on the project in November. A month later, the Oregon State legislature appropriated one hundred thousand dollars to purchase right-

"Telegraph" was one of the speediest passenger packets on the lower Columbia River. When challenged, she could turn up some twenty miles an hour.

of-way for the canal. The State deeded four hundred and seventy-nine acres to the United States in April, 1905.

On October 5, 1905, the long wait of the open river advocates seemed about to be answered with start of construction on the canal. Another ten years were to pass, however, before the first steamboat would use the waterway.

In anticipation of a lengthy construction project, the State of Oregon built a new portage road from Big Eddy to Celilo. It opened in mid-1905 and in 1911 was extended to The Dalles.

Meanwhile, competition from the railroads had forced removal of most of the middle river steamboats. Stern-wheelers still operating on the Snake were primarily connecting with the railheads at Riparia and Pasco. Captain W. P. Gray, old-time steamboat master, commented in his memoirs on the low state of affairs by 1905:

"As soon as the O. R. & N. was completed to Riparia, and the Northern Pacific from Pasco to Tacoma, it began to be asserted that the rivers were too dangerous to navigate and that it was impossible to take a steamboat from Riparia to the mouth of the Snake River.

"This idea proved so prevalent that when in June, 1905, I was preparing to take a party of excursionists on the steamer, "Mountain Gem," from Lewiston to Celilo for the opening of the Oregon State portage road around The Dalles, Senator Heyburn of Idaho asked me if it would be safe for his

"Tahoma" turns into the stream as "Dalles City" makes fast at Warren's salmon cannery on the Oregon shore, just below present Bonneville Dam. Benjamin A. Gifford, commercial photographer of The Dalles, dated the photo 1902.

wife to make the trip, and was surprised when I told him that the river had been navigated for over forty years and at one time carried all the traffic between Portland and Lewiston."

Proponents of the open river project, who had shepherded the Celilo Canal proposal through Congress, organized a navigation company in 1906 to put their own boats on the river above Celilo. The State Portage Road provided the connecting link between the upper and lower river where the "Charles R. Spencer" ran from The Dalles to Portland along with boats of the Regulator Line.

Above Celilo the company placed the "Relief" but she was under-powered and had to be supported by the more capable "Mountain Gem." Eventually the Open River Navigation Company fleet consisted of the "J. N. Teal" between Portland and The Dalles, "Twin Cities" and "Inland Empire," Celilo to Lewiston and the "Relief," Celilo to Pasco.

Navigation improvements, mainly blasting of rock reefs and rapids, were carried on by the Corps of Engineers. In 1911 work at Umatilla Rapids made this stretch more passable during low water periods.

Work on Celilo Canal was going forward. Congress was niggardly in appropriating funds, but so long as the ditch progressed its supporters remained high spirited. For its day, the undertaking was substantial. Involved was removal of one million, four hundred thousand cubic yards of granite and one million, eight hundred thousand cubic yards of gravel and sand. One million pounds of dynamite were used to blast the channel. Of concrete, two hundred thousand yards were required to construct walls through soft earth and sand sections. Numerous passing turnouts were built, although the sixty five foot width and eight foot depth of the eight and one-half mile canal allowed safe passage of even the largest river steamers. The final price was four million, eight hundred and fifty thousand dollars. When the day came to cut the ribbon every dollar and all the long years of waiting seemed worth it.

Opening of the Canal brought rejoicing to every community from Lewiston to Astoria. For the first time the river was completely open, with through navigation from its mouth as far up the Columbia as Priest Rapids and up the Snake to the Grande Ronde.

The full week of May 3, 1915, was devoted to celebration. Historical parades, fireworks, speeches, picnics, special honors to Northwest pioneers — nothing was overlooked as each town vied to outdo the next in appropriate commemoration.

A steamboat fleet, commanded by the pioneer Captain Gray, boarded enthusiastic participants at Lewiston. Stops were made at Pasco and Kennewick, Wallula, Umatilla, Arlington, Maryhill, Big Eddy, The Dalles, (where twenty thousand persons turned out for the festivities), Vancouver, Portland, (for two parades, dinners and orations), Kalama, and Astoria.

A side trip was made to Oregon City

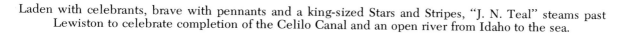

Laden with celebrants, brave with pennants and a king-sized Stars and Stripes, "J. N. Teal" steams past Lewiston to celebrate completion of the Celilo Canal and an open river from Idaho to the sea.

to celebrate transfer of the Willamette Locks from ownership of the Portland Railway, Light & Power Company to the federal government, opening up toll-free navigation on the Willamette.

The official program for the Celilo Canal festivities prophesied: "To the come about slowly and by gradual degrees, but it will come, and the present celebration commemorating the completion of the Celilo canal marks the commencement of a new era of commerce and industry for this section of the great Northwest."

Portland's delegation to the Celilo opening festivites rode the Hosford Transportation Company's "Undine" as she passed through Big Eddy locks.

Inland Empire, the Celilo Canal is relatively of as much importance as is the Panama Canal to the nation as a whole. It will re-establish trade lines; it will mean the revision of railroad tariffs; it will bring new development to the great valley of the Columbia, a territory rich with latent possibilities. This may

The rosy prospect failed to materialize. Though the Columbia at last was open, commercial river operations ground almost completely to a standstill. In the first five years after its opening, Celilo Canal locked through only four thousand, and twenty tons. In 1925 a disappointing two hundred and

Wherever the triumphant fleet docked, throngs shared the historic occasion. At Big Eddy, the Celilo Canal met the portage railroad it had replaced after fifty-two years of service.

nine tons passed. It began to appear Uncle Sam had created one of his more expensive white elephants.

Several attempts were made to generate traffic. The Willamette River Transportation Company and the Oregon City Transportation Company put boats on the run, but business did not warrant the expense. Cascade Locks continued to handle tonnage but most was rafted logs headed for downstream mills. Miscellaneous merchandise that earlier had flowed heavily in

and out of the Inland Empire fell off sharply under the impact of truck and rail competition.

By 1930 the situation had deteriorated so far that the Port of Portland Commission undertook a survey to determine causes and possible remedies. The report pinpointed the problems:

"Insufficient volume of traffic in either direction; lack of concentrated population on the Columbia River above The Dalles; inability to reach

Lewiston because of shallow conditions of the Snake River most of the year; lack of terminals and landing facilities; inability to secure balanced cargoes and to reach and serve localities not immediately on the river; seasonal character of products depended upon for downstream cargoes; inability to give frequent service."

The steamer "Lewiston" waits patiently at the upper entrance of Celilo Canal while repairs are made on a leak in the bottom of the ditch, which caused much of the water to vanish. Captain Fred G. McDermott, long time skipper and owner-operator of numerous river boats, stands on the lock wall.

One steamboat operator stated: "River transportation on the Columbia above Vancouver is not an operating problem. If anyone can secure a volume of traffic in both directions there are plenty of steamboats and operators who will handle that traffic."

A few more years were to pass before the situation improved. In 1932 river men, faced with a glut of spare sternwheelers and Depression prices for wheat, attempted to revive transportation with a new concept. The plan was simple and it worked: form a combination of truck and river haul from the mid-Columbia region to seek lower transportation costs to the Portland elevators. When enough farmers agreed to use the new service to indicate a profitable venture, the firm of Shaver Forwarding Company was formed.

The fleet of powerful diesel tugs and barges that now regularly plies the waterway had its genesis in the minds of a Spokane businessman and a Seattle naval architect who together created the first practical propeller-driven tugboat to combat the Columbia's whitewater conditions.

"Mary Gail" was the first diesel propeller tug on the river, precursor of today's powerful fleet. She entered service between Portland and Attalia in 1937 with a dual purpose barge — petroleum up, grain down.

Strictly a working girl, "Vulcan" seldom took time off for a paint job.

mand of Captain Stewart V. Winslow, veteran pilot whose career thus spanned the transition from stern-wheel packet to diesel-driven work-horse.

Two years later, on February 20, 1939, the second phase of the new era was ushered in. On that day, from the Port Kelley elevator of Walla Walla Grain Growers, the "Mary Gail" nudged the first commercial barge load of bulk grain into the Columbia's current and pointed her nose downstream. This six thousand bushel shipment was the forerunner of the tremendous traffic now moving on the waterway.

The boat was the "Mary Gail," slightly more than fifty-six feet long, diesel powered, and with two propellers. Her draft was shallow, necessitated by fluctuating river levels in the years before dams flooded the hazards of rock and reef between the head of Bonneville Dam pool and the mouth of the Snake.

Kirk Thompson, of Spokane, saw in the "Mary Gail" the answer to revival of the Columbia's historic river traffic. He drew the specifications and employed Seattle marine designer H. C. Hansen to complete the concept. The craft was launched in Seattle in November, 1936. Off the ways with her came the Pacific Coast's first all-welded steel barge with a petroleum carrying capacity of one hundred thousand gallons.

By early 1937, the "Mary Gail" was in regular service between Portland and Attalia, Washington, under com-

Under the shadow of the Steel Bridge and hard by the river, the Boss Lunch stood for two generations until displaced by construction of Harbor Drive. Hangout of steamboatmen, foremast hands, and assorted waterfront characters, it was also headquarters for crimps. Rumor had it that a tunnel connected the basement to the river, where rowboats waited on dark nights to transport unwilling seamen to short-handed windship skippers. Perfumed, beribboned diversions were offered on the second floor.

With the practicality of river transportation assured by operations of Shaver Forwarding Company and by Kirk Thompson's vision and enterprise, attention turned toward further improvements to navigation. Construction of Bonneville Dam, with a lock seventy-six feet wide and five hundred feet long, was begun in 1933. It was completed five years later, drowning out Cascade Locks and backing a slack-water pool to The Dalles.

Such projects had been the concern of Columbia River communities for many years. Citizen groups had beaten the drums for numerous dam sites: Umatilla, Wallula, Arlington. Each town had its favored scheme. Congress and the federal agencies involved in river development planning were regularly petitioned with fevered pleas.

The start on Bonneville coalesced regional sentiment under the banner of the Inland Empire Waterways

Portland's west side waterfront between the Broadway and Hawthorne bridges throbbed with the comings and goings of dozens of paddle wheelers. In this turn of the century scene, the "N. R. Lang" goes sedately about her business.

Lower harbor of Portland, from the Broadway Bridge, July, 1924.

Association, which formed in 1934. In the years that followed, an orderly program of dam development emerged. Today, the Columbia and Snake Rivers are all but canalized between the head of tidewater at Vancouver and the present end of navigation at Lewiston. Across the once-turbulent rivers have been flung the multiple-purpose dams of Bonneville, The Dalles, John Day, McNary, Ice Harbor and Lower Monumental. Work is underway on Little Goose and Lower Granite.

And as the dams changed the pattern of transportation, so river equipment changed with it. Diesel tugs may not be as handsome as stately stern-wheelers, but they are far more efficient and less expensive to operate. Powerful enough to fight their way through the remaining fast water, pushing two or more barges ahead, they have become today's familiar link between the upriver ports and the deepwater docks of Portland, Vancouver, Kalama, Longview, and Astoria.

The fierce competition of the earlier days also has passed away. In 1944, Shaver Forwarding Company and Tidewater Transportation Company merged as Tidewater-Shaver Barge Lines. The river fleet under the merger included the "Invader," "Defiance," "Viking," and "Captain Al James." These shortly were joined by a new "Mary Gail," built to replace the original boat which had been damaged by fire. Tidewater-Shaver Barge Lines served the river until 1956, when the name became Tidewater Barge Lines, under which it now operates.

Prominent also in this period was Inland Navigation Company, incorporated at Seattle in 1935. The tug, "Mystic," was brought from Grays Harbor to the Columbia as first vessel in a fleet that finally numbered eleven towboats and small river craft and twenty-five barges. In 1959, ownership of Inland Navigation Company and its affiliate, Upper Columbia River Towing Company, passed to the newly-formed Pacific Inland Navigation Company.

Thus an era ended. Today, of half a thousand stern-wheelers that plied the waters of the Columbia and Snake and their tributaries during the past hundred years, only the steamer "Portland" remains on active duty as the reminder of a vanished day. But every once in a while she is called into service and the soft splash of her paddle wheel, the plume of white steam from her tall black stack, and the unmistakeable tocsin of her throaty whistle are reminders of a day when the pace was less frenzied, and there was time to enjoy the passing scene.

Following collision and sinking in the lower Columbia River in March, 1937, the Italian steamship "Feltre" is assisted to Portland for drydocking and repairs by the "Portland" and "Umatilla."

Above left: "Pomona" herds two hog fuel barges in Portland Harbor. *Above right*: "Lurline" ran opposite "T. J. Potter," "Georgiana," and other Portland-Astoria steamers. *Bottom*: The O. W. R. & N. packet, "Harvest Queen," at the Altoona, Washington, cannery dock.

A fine freight and towing boat, "F. B. Jones" worked the lower Columbia for thirty-six years.

The Ilwaco Railway and Navigation Company steamer "Ocean Wave," flanked by her officers. The side-wheeler, built in 1891, served the beach trade between Portland and Ilwaco, Washington, near the mouth of the Columbia.

"Skookum," built at Aberdeen for log towing on Grays Harbor, later transferred to the Columbia for Milton Smith of Rainier. In Chinook jargon "skookum" translates as strong.

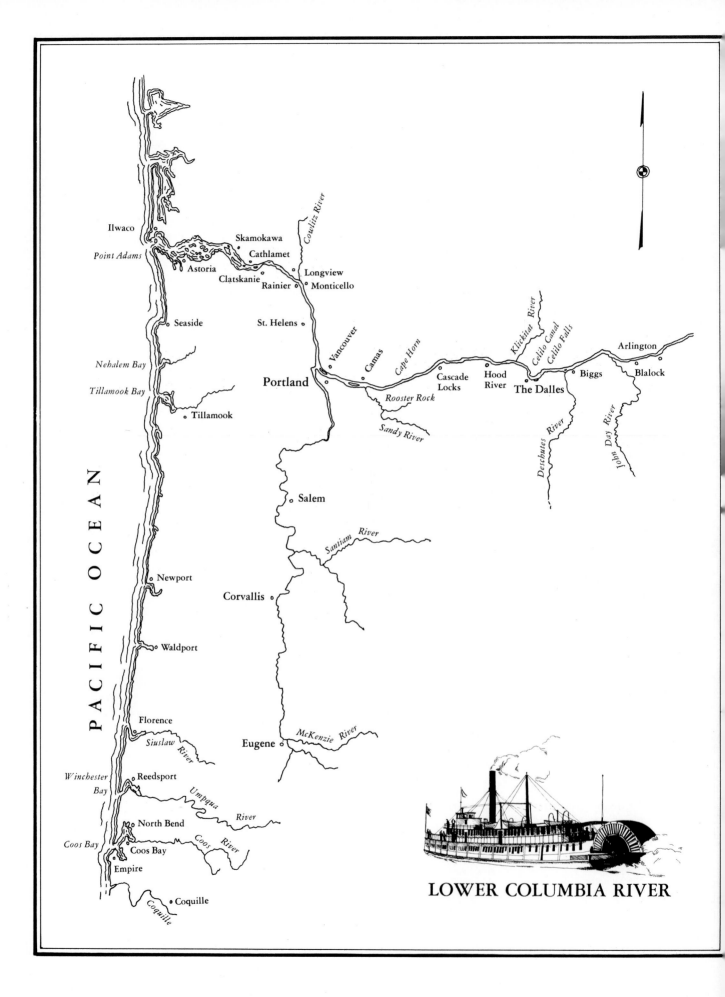

PACIFIC OCEAN

Ilwaco
Point Adams
Seaside
Nehalem Bay
Tillamook Bay
Tillamook
Newport
Waldport
Florence
Siuslaw River
Winchester Bay
Reedsport
Umpqua River
North Bend
Coos Bay
Coos Bay
Coos River
Empire
Coquille
Coquille

Skamokawa
Cathlamet
Astoria
Clatskanie
Rainier
St. Helens
Longview
Monticello
Cowlitz River

Portland
Vancouver
Camas
Cape Horn
Rooster Rock
Sandy River

Salem
Santiam River
Corvallis
McKenzie River
Eugene

Cascade Locks
Hood River
The Dalles
Klickitat River
Celilo Canal
Celilo Falls
Biggs
Arlington
Blalock
Deschutes River
John Day River

LOWER COLUMBIA RIVER

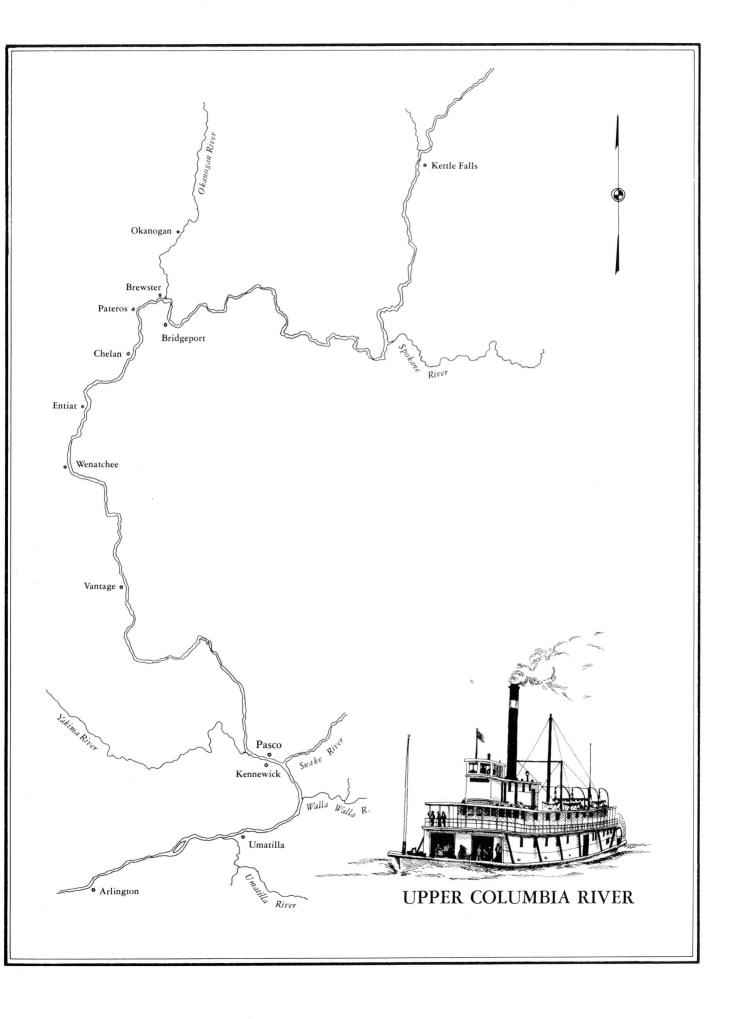

Kettle Falls

Okanogan

Brewster
Pateros
Bridgeport
Chelan

Entiat

Wenatchee

Vantage

Okanogan River

Spokane River

Yakima River

Pasco
Kennewick

Snake River

Walla Walla R.

Umatilla

Umatilla River

Arlington

UPPER COLUMBIA RIVER

"Okanogan" meets the stagecoach at Chelan Falls.

Brewster Landing, sixty-five miles above Wenatchee.

In 1910 at Bridgeport, Washington, passengers lounge over the rail as deckhands labor and the captain waits patiently in his pilot house.

The scow-like "Bridgeport" labored from 1917 until 1942 in the Bridgeport, Brewster, and Pateros reach of the upper Columbia, hauling boxed fruit, sacked flour and grain, and box shook to the Pateros railhead from numerous river landings.

A crowd of weekend excursionists gives the little "Gerome" a welcome break from humdrum daily freight hauling. "Gerome" was home-ported at Wenatchee for the Columbia River & Okanogan Steamboat Company.

THE COLUMBIA RIVER STERN-WHEELER — A TYPE

To the eye of many beholders, there was beauty in the Columbia River type stern-wheeler. Her hull lines were graceful, clean and shallow, and about five times longer than the beam. The slight dead-rise made for a flat deck. The lower deck was housed forward from the wheel, with the forward doors and those on the guards wide enough for freight or engine and boiler parts. Above was the cabin deck, with a wide, railed promenade all around, a central passenger lounge and dining room and windowed saloons fore and aft. The upper, or hurricane deck, carried a texas, with crew cabins or passenger accommodations. Atop the texas and well forward was the pilot house. This

"Hercules" (ex-"Staghound") shows clean lines of a typical paddle wheeler as she awaits launching at Dan Kerns' boatyard, foot of East Market Street, Portland.

When "Staghound" snapped her hog chains off the Columbia bar in an attempt to tow her to Alaska, she was rebuilt as the towboat "Hercules."

was the Holy of Holies, grandly occupied by the Captain and Pilot, with lesser mortals granted admission only by special dispensation. Three sides of the pilot house bore gracefully carved name boards. Often fancy fretwork topped it all.

Aft of the pilot house rose the single stack. The kingpost soared amidships, flanked by at least four hog posts to which were secured the hog chains that keep the supple hull aligned. After 1870, the stern-wheel often was enclosed in a box on which appeared the craft's name and port of registry and which also served to keep spray off the passengers.

The main deck forward was open for winches and capstans and cargo.

Wood construction was favored, even after steel became available. Initial cost and upkeep of wooden hulls were cheaper. Damage repair was easy — a soft patch spiked over a broken plank kept the boat afloat until it could reach the beach.

For propulsion, early engineers preferred a high-pressure, non-condensing engine. Cylinder bores varied between ten and twenty-two inches and the piston stroke was six or seven

The low, powerful lines of a stern-wheel towboat are evident on "Wauna" of 1906, built for Lake River log towing. She later handled oil barges on the Willamette until her layup in 1937.

feet, rarely more. Locomotive-type boilers had a working pressure of about one hundred pounds per square inch. Not until well after World War I did cross-compound engines appear. These engines transmitted relatively low but effective power to the wheel and so were often provided with a by-pass valve to permit fast injection of live steam into the low-pressure boiler in case the pilot called for extra power in a hurry. A few tandem-compound power plants were built. Among these was the "Henderson" at the time of her 1929 rebuild.

A sleek, trim stern-wheeler, moving grandly through a covey of noisy, bustling steam tugs, had a never-to-be-forgotten air about her whether she was a fast passenger packet or a towboat. Sure enough, they don't make 'em like that anymore.

Launching of "Wauna," in 1906.

INCIDENT AT THE MADISON ST. BRIDGE

"Elwood," built at Portland in 1891.

The little stern-wheel steamer "Elwood" groped her way up the Willamette River toward Portland's Madison Street bridge through blanketing river fog. In the wheelhouse, the pilot shivered against the November morning's frost. He pulled the whistle cord, a long and three shorts for the drawspan, and rang the engineer to stop the engines. The bridge tender acknowledged and swung shut the bridge gates; the span slowly creaked open to pass the "Elwood" through.

At the throttle of the town-bound

Hawthorne trolley, the motorman eased back a few notches to check the speed picked up on the downgrade to the bridge. As he peered through the fog, he saw the barrier and the open draw. He pushed the control lever to full off and wound on the hand brake to stop the car. The wheels locked, then slid like sled runners on the frosty rails.

The barrier's wood snapped into slivers; for an instant of time the car hung on the edge, then it slipped slowly over into the river. It barely missed the steamer.

There was nothing the pilot could do as the "Elwood" drifted over the circle of bubbles where the car had been. He couldn't start his engines. The paddle wheel would strike survivors struggling in the water. He could only wait until he was clear of the bridge to turn back and help. Rowboats were there by then, and twenty who struggled free of the car were pulled into them and onto the "Elwood." Seven did not make it.

The "Elwood" was built in 1891 for the Oregon Railway and Navigation Company for the Portland-Oregon City shuttle run. She was of light draft to pass the rapids at the mouth of the Clackamas River and, with her younger sister boat the "Elmore," became popular on the route.

Competition must have been unprofitable, for in 1894 she was sold to the Lewis River Transportation Company and put into service on the Lewis River-Lake River route. In 1903, she was running for new owners between Seattle and Tacoma. There the "Elwood's" history ends.

Stern-wheelers like the "Elwood" and the trolley cars of Portland are items of curiosity now, suitable for enshrining as mementos of a slower-paced day. But if you stand at the right place at the Willamette seawall and listen closely in a frosty, foggy Portland dawn you might hear the muffled hoot of a steamboat whistle and the whine of steel sliding on steel, a splintering crash and then — nothing.

"JENNIE CLARK," TREND SETTER

At the start, Columbia river steamboats copied traditional hull designs and propulsion systems that had proved their worth on the waterways of the eastern seaboard and of the Mississippi river and its tributaries. These boats were driven by side-wheels or propellers and when the builders

"Oneonta" was built Mississippi River style. The Oregon Steam Navigation Company had her on the middle river run between the Cascades and The Dalles.

"Jennie Clark."

moved to the Oregon country they transplanted their knowledge and experience to its rivers.

But propellers broke shafts or bent on uncharted rocks or were immobilized by shallow water. Sidewheels were inefficient and difficult to maneuver in fast and shifting currents.

Builders and captains wrestled with the problem from the day of the "Beaver" in 1836 until the fertile imagination of Jacob Kamm provided the answer in 1855. It appeared in the form of the "Jennie Clark," first stern-wheeler on the Columbia River and trend-setter of a construction style that has existed with only minor modifications to the present.

Putting the paddle wheel on the stern close by the rudders was a stroke of genius. Maneuverability was immeasurably better. Two engines,

each with a cylinder of four foot stroke connected to the wheel by a sixteen foot rod, provided the power.

The "Jennie Clark" proved to be fast and comfortable. Under the command of Captain J. C. Ainsworth, she carried the daily mail between Portland and Oregon City. The captain and Abernathy and Clark Co., for whom Kamm had built the boat, owned one-fourth shares in the "Jennie Clark" and Kamm retained a half interest. Later, Theodore Wygant purchased Captain Ainsworth's share and Kamm sold a three-sixteenths share to Captain Josiah Myrick, who then took command of the boat.

Eventually, ownership of the "Jennie Clark" passed to the river's greatest monopoly, the Oregon Steam Navigation Co. Under their flag, the boat established another "first." In

1862, she inaugurated the "seaside" run, making a weekly trip between Portland and Fort Clatsop Landing on the Lewis and Clark River across Young's Bay from Astoria.

This was the start of the beach excursions that for the next couple of generations were immensely popular with Portlanders and which brought into full flower the Oregon coast resort communities of Seaside and Gearhart, and Seaview, Long Beach, and Ocean Park on the Washington peninsula.

A round trip on the "Jennie Clark" cost fifteen dollars and beach accommodations were primitive at the outset. But this was new adventure, and nobody really minded the cost or the inconvenience.

By 1865 the "Jennie Clark" was retired from service, her engines going in the "Forty-Nine," built at Little Dalles on the upper Columbia near the forty-ninth parallel, from which the steamboat derived her name.

Though her career was short and relatively uneventful, the "Jennie Clark" deserves a larger place in history than she usually is given. She set a trend that was to prevail for the next hundred years and which resulted in a type of river craft suited uniquely to the times and the purpose.

NOT ALWAYS PRETTY, BUT THEY RAN

Columbia River steamboat men were, often as not, an opinionated lot little given to seeking advice and, when it was offered, not inclined to follow it. Among the more independent was Captain U. B. Scott, who steamboated on the Ohio from 1859 until 1873 when he came to Oregon. He needed a job and offered his services to the People's Transportation Company and the Oregon Steam Navigation Company. Both turned him down. They came to regret this rashness, for Captain Scott with two financial backers and a pile of dredge machinery, proceeded to go into business for himself. The result

Steamer "Ohio."

was the "Ohio," first "light draft" steamer in the Northwest. She was one hundred and forty feet long but drew only eight inches. Captain Scott had built the "Ohio" like a barge. Scoffers, coming to look at her on the ways, took Scott's backers aside and extended sympathy, suggesting that if they went through with the venture they didn't stand to lose too much money; Captain Scott was building pretty economically.

Indeed he was. The pitmans were of gas pipe which sometimes bent when strained, making it impossible to move the wheel. This resulted in embarrasing collisions with docks. Her stern-wheel was of wood, since Captain Scott had dispensed with the iron circles commonly used to hold the wheel together. Under pressure, segments of the wheel would drop off, stopping the steamer. A deckhand would be called to lower a boat and row after the pieces which had to be replaced before the "Ohio" could proceed.

But after her first trip in December 1874, when Captain Scott herded the "Ohio" up the Willamette to Eugene, the scoffers ate their words. He came back down to Portland with seventy tons of wheat and her shallow draft permitted her to get forty miles beyond any river landing accessible to rival steamers. Within the first three months, the "Ohio" had cleared ten thousand dollars and check-waving backers were fighting each other to offer money to finance Captain Scott's next vessel.

During the same year another floating curiosity appeared in British Columbia waters. This was the "Union," composed of a flat-bottomed scow propelled by side-wheels connected by chain drive to a threshing machine engine. Since the engine had no reversing gear, the "Union" had to drift into a landing with the aid of a pike pole and line. When leaving a dock, a long sweep and the pike pole were used to head her in the right direction.

The "Union" operated for many years, through several ownerships. Toward the end, when the hull had become quite tender, it was usual to fasten a stout chain around the engine, to which was attached a line and buoy, so the machinery might be found should it drop through the bottom while on a trip.

OPEN RIVER

First by-pass of obstructions to free river travel came at Willamette Falls with opening of a canal and locks in early 1873. The Willamette Falls Canal and Locks Company, Associated, completed its ditch on the west bank ahead of its rival, the Peoples Transportation Company, which tackled the east side.

Navigation along many stretches of the Columbia River in the steamboat days was, even under the best of conditions, a chancy thing. The river was cluttered by rapids at several places, and the worst were Celilo and the Cascades. Other tough stretches, such as Umatilla Rapids, gave passengers and pilots the willies, especially during certain low water stages. But at Celilo and the Cascades, no vessel could pass upstream. Very few, piloted by only the most daring captains, dared run down and then only at high water.

So for many years the steamboat lines relied on portage railways past these obstructions, with passengers and freight hauled around to a waiting transfer boat.

The demand for an open river — a

With the opening of the Willamette Falls canal, the Locks Company's "E. N. Cooke" and "Success" promptly solicited passengers and freight for upriver points.

river free of impediments to navigation from its mouth to its farthest reaches — had been raised since the earliest days. But since the steamboat companies were satisfied with their profitable portage railroads and Congress was reluctant to appropriate money to build canals, little was done until

Colonel Joseph Teal took up the cudgel.

Colonel Teal ran a general store in Eugene, some one hundred twenty-five miles up the Willamette from Portland. He turned his energies first to the problem of locks past Willamette Falls at Oregon City so steamboats could reach the landing that served his store. This job was accomplished in 1873. With that under his belt, the Colonel focused on the Cascades, and saw that canal through to completion by the government in 1896.

That left only Celilo, and Colonel Teal passed the torch on to his son, Joseph N. Teal, who was filled with the same open river zeal as his father. Behind him gathered all the force of the Portland Chamber of Commerce, the Open River Association, and group after group interested in breaking the barrier of Celilo and crushing the monopoly of the portages.

Meanwhile, steamboats of the Open River Navigation Company and

The rock-studded channel through the Cascades was six miles of potential disaster. In 1888, Captain James Troup drove "Hassalo" through the rapids in seven minutes, giving the spectators almost as much of a thrill as he gave the passengers.

"Inland Empire" (foreground) and "Undine" in the Big Eddy basin, Celilo Canal.

Regulator Line began to offer serious competition to the Union Pacific, owner of the rail line which paralleled the Columbia River's south bank, and which drained the extensive wheat trade away from the competing steamboats.

The Open River Company's third boat was the "J. N. Teal," named after that staunch exponent of the open river campaign. She was launched in 1906 at Portland, burned almost at once, was rebuilt and ready for service in 1908. With a lower river fleet and connecting boats above Celilo, steamboating on the Columbia witnessed a revival and the railroad faced stiff competition.

Surveys for the Celilo Canal were finished by now and work began. In April, 1915, the "J. N. Teal" and the "Inland Empire" passed through it upbound, the first vessels to cruise the open river. Mr. Joseph N. Teal made the dedicatory oration using the same soaring rhetoric as had his father at the opening of Willamette Locks forty-two years before.

So the rivers were freed of barriers. In the years since, dams and locks have made them freer still, until now the Columbia is slack water to Pasco and the Snake River dams will soon end all hazards to navigation as far as Lewiston, Idaho.

AMONG THOSE MISSING . . .

Steamboat explosions on the Columbia, Snake, and Willamette Rivers were no rarity; most had tragic results and the loss of life from explosion and fire often was substantial.

One of the worst also was one of the earliest. The side-wheeler "Gazelle" was loading freight at six o'clock one morning in April, 1858, at Canemah, a short distance above Willamette Falls. Smoke spiraled idly from her stack and passengers lounged over the rail to watch the work. Suddenly the engineer rushed for the gangway, and hit the bank on a dead run.

In another minute the "Gazelle's"

On a bold rock outcropping overlooking old Canemah Landing, a simple plaque commemorates the first major steamboat disaster in the Pacific Northwest, the wreck of "Gazelle." The marker reads: 600 yards south of this point — Explosion of Steamer Gazelle, April 8th, 1854. Loss of twenty-four lives. Marked May 18th, 1933 by Multnomah Chapter D.A.R.

"State of Washington" originally was a Puget Sound boat that also served in a variety of trades on the Columbia. Her end came in a boiler explosion off Tongue Point in 1920 while towing an oil barge.

Wreck of "State of Washington."

boiler blew up, the upper works disintegrated in a roar of high-pressure steam, and bodies and cargo were hurled in all directions. Townspeople came running. Men rushed to the wreckage, tugging out bodies and laying them on the bank. Others jumped into rowboats to bring injured and dead out of the water.

There was nothing left of the "Gazelle" but the hull, and under the debris there were more bodies. The tally showed twenty-four were killed and some of the thirty wounded were dying.

The coroner's jury met to ask questions, but the engineer had kept moving until he was out of the Territory. The captain was cleared and the blame finally was placed on the chief engineer for gross negligence in knowingly carrying more steam pressure than was safe and for neglecting to keep sufficient water in the boilers.

The explosion of the little sternwheeler "Elk" three years later entered into the folklore of the Willamette River. Just below the mouth of the Yamhill her boiler turned loose and lifted itself skyward, taking cabin, captain, and smokestack with it. Captain Jerome later said he had looked down through the stack to see his pilot sitting on the bank. The captain arced gracefully through the air to land in a cottonwood tree. Captain Jerome shinnied down to the ground, and for twenty years pilots along the river pointed out the tree and related the story of his adventure.

End of the big stern-wheeler "Annie Faxon" on April 14, 1893, came from a boiler explosion in which eight died. Her regular freight-passenger run was on the Snake River, touching at landings below Lewiston. At Wade's Bar, Captain Harry Baughman pulled the whistle cord and headed in to pick up a bit of freight and a lone passenger. Purser Tappan left his cabin, where his new bride sat, to collect the dollar fare and check the manifest. As the "Annie Faxon" neared the bank, Captain Baughman rang down the engines. Almost immediately there was a low, ominous rumble from below decks and the cabin of the steamboat collapsed upon itself.

Purser Tappan turned to speak to a deckhand standing by the gangway and saw him dead on the deck. Captain Baughman's pilot was beheaded by a sliver of flying wreckage, and the Captain a moment later found himself dazed and injured on the bank, blown there by the explosion.

Purser Tappan survived, but not his bride, who was thrown into the river and drowned.

Wreck of the "Annie Faxon."

Steamer "Annie Faxon," built in 1877 by Oregon Steam Navigation Co.

TROUBLE ON THE MIDDLE RIVER

The pioneering days of Columbia River steamboating offered much more than humdrum hauling of freight and passengers. Fires, floods, boiler explosions, collisions, and sinkings were taken in stride. But even such diversions as these paled by comparison with the long-remembered Indian uprising at the Cascades.

It was 1856. Indians throughout the Northwest had been restless for a couple of years, jumping the reservation for sporadic raids, and making other, mainly futile, efforts to stem the tide of whites. The Army maintained a garrison at The Dalles, some eighty miles up the Columbia from Vancouver. In 1855 a blockhouse had been erected at Middle Cascades to protect residents of Bradford's Landing and the crews building a six-mile portage railroad between Lower and Upper Cascades on the Washington shore.

Two competing steamboat companies served the river at the time. The rivals "Belle" and "Fashion" ran between Portland and the foot of the rapids; at the portage they connected with the "Mary" and "Wasco." The "Belle-Mary" Line used the north bank portage, the "Fashion-Wasco" Line the south, or Oregon, connection.

On a day in late March, the "Mary" and the "Wasco" dropped down from The Dalles to their Cascades terminal to load upbound cargo. The work went on through the afternoon and resumed again next morning. Both boats, the "Mary" at Bradford's Landing and the "Wasco" across the river at the pack trail's upper end, had damped their fires. Without warning, shots rang out and Indians closed in on Bradford's store. Her crew raced from shore for the "Mary," grabbed guns, and fought off the hostiles while the engineer got steam up. As soon as the pressure rose, the "Mary" pulled away and ran upstream to wood up. The Indians retired to besiege the store where the settlers had sought refuge. Across the river, the "Wasco's" crew heard the fracas and rushed to fire up her boilers. Soon the two boats, safety valves tied down, were racing for The Dalles and help.

Meantime, a friendly Indian paddled downriver by canoe to Fort Vancouver with word of the attack. Lieutenant Philip Sheridan assembled his dragoons and commandeered the "Belle." At daylight the next morning he headed for the scene, arriving in the afternoon at the lower landing to find everything burned. Sheridan landed his troops, met resistance, and forted up for the night. The next morning he moved on to Bradford's. With the arrival at the upper landing of soldiers from The Dalles on the "Mary" and

"Wasco," and with Sheridan's force moving in on them from below, the Indians were pinched off. They abandoned the fight and slipped away into the forest.

The toll was sixteen civilians and soldiers dead, twelve wounded. But the back of Indian resistance was broken and the "Belle" and "Fashion," the "Mary" and "Wasco" could go about their business.

Courtesy Oregon Historical Society

The middle blockhouse, site of the Indian attack.

FIRE IN THE NIGHT

When Captain Alexander Griggs turned his back on the Mississippi where he had learned the steamboating trade along with his good friend Mark Twain, it was to head for the newer, more challenging waters of the Columbia River. The Captain liked his steamboating tough. He didn't bother about the lower or middle Columbia where all the white water had been conquered. Captain Griggs traveled direct to Wenatchee, four hundred and sixty-five miles from the Columbia's mouth, and the point from which all upbound travelers left the railroad and boarded the boats to their destinations.

Captain Griggs got what he was looking for. From Wenatchee to the mouth of the Okanogan, some seventy miles above, the Columbia had few stretches of slackwater where a steamboat could take it easy. The river was a series of boils, sandbars, reefs and rapids and the only difference among them was that some were nastier than others. The cooperative Corps of Engineers had dynamited the more obvious rocks and snags. But the Corps' biggest contribution had been installation of ring bolts at strategic points. To these lines could be attached whereby a steamboat could winch itself up to better water, literally

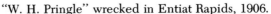

"W. H. Pringle" wrecked in Entiat Rapids, 1906.

"W. H. Pringle," deck loaded with cordwood fuel, idles at the Wenatchee wharfboat as "Columbia" swings in for a landing.

hand over hand. If there were no ring bolts, or if a freshet temporarily kicked up a stretch of water beyond the boat's power to buck, her skipper resorted to a simpler method. He pulled over to the bank and sent a deckhand in search of an accommodating farmer. A couple of teams of horses then would drag the craft through the bad part, helped out by the steamboat's engines.

In 1893, a couple of years after his arrival at Wenatchee, Captain Griggs formed the Columbia & Okanogan Steamboat Co. Soon he had eight boats on the river, hauling settlers and supplies into new lands being opened by the railroads in the Okanogan Valley and the Big Bend country.

Casualties on the run were high. Captain Griggs lost the "Alexander Griggs" and the "W. H. Pringle" in Entiat Rapids. The "Selkirk" went to pieces at Rock Island Rapids. But for some time business was good and the C. & O. S. Co. made money. The fleet remained in service until about 1910, when the pace of settlement slowed. Captain Griggs was forced to sell off his boats until by 1915 only four remained, the "Columbia," "North Star," "Chelan," and "Okanogan."

With trade dormant, Captain Griggs

Biggest and best-appointed of the upper Columbia River fleet was "Okanogan," built in 1907 and burned in 1915 in Wenatchee's most disastrous waterfront fire. The slowly turning wheel holds her nose against the Brewster wharfboat.

foreman checked the vessels at eleven P.M., and again at one A. M. Satisfied all was well, he went to sleep in the carpenter shop, fifty yards away. At two-twenty A.M., the night pumpman at the Fifth Street pumping station, saw flames licking from the "North Star." Within two minutes all four tinder dry boats were a seething mass of flames, and by the time firemen arrived they only could turn their efforts toward saving buildings on shore. The "Columbia," "Okanogan," and "North Star" burned to the water's edge, their engines falling through the bottoms into the river. The "Chelan" was damaged beyond repair. Since all possible precautions had been taken against fire, since the yard foreman who had been working on the "North Star" did not smoke and was sure no oily waste had been left on board, arson was suspected but never proved.

The loss ended the Columbia & Okanogan Steamboat Company. Insurance on the boats had expired a short while before and Captain Griggs was waiting sale of the "North Star" to get enough money to renew the policy.

tied his boats to a barge at the bank at Wenatchee. They were lying abreast, the "Chelan" closest inshore, the "North Star" on the outside. The latter was to be delivered in a few days to a new owner, Captain Fred McDermott, who planned to take her up to Bridgeport.

On the night of July 8th the boatyard

"Chelan" at the Okanogan landing in 1904.

TRAGIC END OF THE "DAISY AINSWORTH"

The night of November 22, 1876, was raw and blustery. Snow squalls rode the wind and no moon offered relief from the oppressive darkness. At The Dalles landing deckhands prodded and cursed, driving the last of two hundred and ten head of beef cattle across a slippery gangway to the lower deck of the "Daisy Ainsworth." From his pilot house window, Martin Spelling watched the scene, lit by small circles of fitful light cast by coal oil lanterns swinging in the raw wind. Spelling reached for the speaking tube and whistled to the engine room. He cautioned Engineer William Doran to stand by and pulled the whistle cord for the warning signal.

For the "Daisy Ainsworth" this would be an unscheduled run. It was the day for a regular trip of the side-wheeler "Idaho," but she was too small to handle the Portland-bound cattle shipment and the "Daisy" had drawn the assignment. John McNulty, captain since her launching on every trip of the "Daisy" but this, would bring mail and passengers down in the morning on the "Idaho." By the time she arrived, the cattle would have been hauled by railroad around the Cascades portage to the waiting transfer boat for the run to Portland.

Captain McNulty had no qualms about turning his command over to Martin Spelling. The young mate knew the river, and Captain McNulty had confidence in his skill and judgment. He was aware, too, that Spelling loved the "Daisy" almost as much as himself.

This elegant steamer, product of master builder John Holland, was pride of the Oregon Steam Navigation Co. fleet. President J. C. Ainsworth had named her in honor of his youngest daughter and had taken the wheel on the "Daisy's" trial run in the spring of 1873. As first of the O.S.N. palace boats on the middle river, the stern-wheeler's appointment boasted every luxury. Cabins and staterooms were carpeted with the finest Brussels. Silver plate adorned dining saloon tables and sideboards; crystal chandeliers glittered with cheerful candle light.

But no passengers are aboard tonight as Captain Spelling rings "Full Ahead" and the vessel swings away from the landing. The pilot house is dark, curtains drawn to shield against distracting glare from the running lights. Ahead are no range markers, no lighted buoys, but Captain Spelling knows the channel.

The "Daisy" passes Crates Point and Captain Spelling puts the wheel over to cross to the Washington channel and avoid the sand bar opposite Cayuse Rock. In the darkness laced with snow squalls driven by the bitter wind howl-

"Daisy Ainsworth."

ing up the Columbia Gorge, the stern-wheeler drives on. It sweeps past Memaloose Island, skirts Mosier Rocks, and threads through the treacherous channel between Eighteen Mile Island and the main shore. Hood River, White Salmon, and Underwood lie in darkness. At intervals, Captain Spelling sounds the whistle to check his distance from shore. The sudden noise further excites the frightened cattle.

Now it is almost two in the morning and Captain Spelling knows he is nearing the end of his forty-five mile run. He peers into the night, looking for the lantern that marks the wharfboat at Upper Cascades. Suddenly and without warning there is a shuddering crash and Captain Spelling pitches forward against the wheel. The splendid "Daisy Ainsworth," her back broken, is impaled on a rock reef not more than three hundred feet above the falls of the Cascades.

In the confusion, the cattle stampede, and many are crowded overboard to drown. A few swim to the bank. The crew huddles on the wreck until daylight when they make their way ashore in a small boat. Then what happened becomes clear. Captain Spelling had mistaken a light on a wood scow moored to the Oregon shore for that of the landing and, in an attempt to cross over to the Washington side, the "Daisy" had been caught by wind and current and swept onto the reef.

Captain Ainsworth spoke no word of criticism to Martin Spelling. But within a few months the grief-stricken man, broken in spirit and in health, was dead. Tuberculosis, said the medical report. But some know the cause was a broken heart.

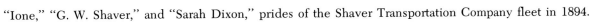

As the blurb says, "G. W. Shaver" stopped at all the landings. She did so for a number of years, first carrying passengers and freight on the Clatskanie route and later handling Astoria traffic.

"Ione," "G. W. Shaver," and "Sarah Dixon," prides of the Shaver Transportation Company fleet in 1894.

"Sarah Dixon" entering Cascade Locks.

One of the most perfectly appointed steamers, "Sarah Dixon" (1892) was outfitted with electric lights, steam steering gear and hoisting engines and superior passenger accommodations.

"G. W. Shaver" of 1889, through transformations became "Glenola" in 1905 and "Beaver" in 1906. She was not a two-stacker; an unidentified steamer is lying behind her at the Couch Street dock.

"G. W. Shaver" with a load of shingles
from Clatskanie, 1899.

Dressed to the nines, captain and crew of "G. W. Shaver" pause for a portrait on an 1897 outing at Latourell
Falls. The lone lady is Mrs. Shaver, wife of Captain Del, at whose knee she sits.

CASE OF THE VANISHING STEAMBOAT

"Zephyr," taken when she was afloat.

For a long time the "Zephyr" was a familiar sight on upper Puget Sound. One of the first stern-wheelers on those waters, she paddled dutifully about her chores through a number of ownerships for twenty-six years. Launched at Seattle in 1871, the "Zephyr" went at once into the Seattle-Olympia passenger and freight trade. So long as she paid strict attention to this responsibility her days were prosaic. It was when she became too slow and unappealing to compete with the newer, more popular passenger packets that her troubles began.

Take that time at Shelton, for example. . . .

The "Zephyr" had been converted to a log raft tug in 1887 but for a few months prior to this metamorphosis she was reduced to the status of water boat. With large tanks installed on her freight deck, she wallowed back and forth across Tacoma harbor supplying fresh water to big square riggers in for cargoes of lumber and grain. The tanks remained on board when she took up her towing work.

At Shelton one evening, just before

he departed for the bright lights uptown, the "Zephyr's" engineer gave careful instructions to his novice fireman. He was to see to it there was plenty of water in the boilers for the next day's run. The fireman nodded agreeably, connected a hose from a dock-side hydrant, and turned on the water pressure. Then he stopped to ponder the inequity of his lot. The rest of the crew were enjoying themselves; surely he had time for a couple of beers while the tanks were filling. But time slipped by and the "Zephyr's" crew returned . . . to an empty berth. They agreed this was where their boat should be, but where was she now? Their consternation mounted until someone looked over the bullrail. A tell-tale gurgling rose beside the dock at the point where a throbbing hose disappeared beneath the water's surface.

The "Zephyr's" boiler had enough water, all right. And so did the tanks. They had filled far beyond the boat's capacity to handle the weight and the "Zephyr's" only solution had been to sink slowly to the bottom of the bay.

Shortly thereafter the "Zephyr" tried another mild protest at her fall from favor as a passenger boat. It happened on a Christmas Eve as the old stern-wheeler paddled solemnly along close to shore. The pilot, overtaken by an excess of holiday fervor, dropped off to sleep at the wheel. The balance of the hands peacefully snored away in the bunks below. With the dawn, the horror-stricken crew looked out not at blue Puget Sound waters but at a land-scape blighted by mud flats. The "Zephyr" was serenely motionless. And there she stayed all during Christmas Day until the tide came back in and floated her off. The chastened crew elected to spend the holiday behind drawn curtains, for the "Zephyr" perversely had chosen as her resting place the approaches to the saw-mill which owned her.

COWLITZ RIVER REMINISCENSES

Back in the days of free-wheeling enterprise and cutthroat competition more than one transportation line was formed by groups of angry farmers and small merchants with craws full of rate gouging and indifferent service by steamboat monopolies.

Rivers were the best means of travel in most parts of the Pacific Northwest until well after the turn of the 1900s.

The Lewis, Lake, Cowlitz, and other small rivers saw much of "Lucea Mason" (1883), a jobbing boat which sank a lot but made considerable money for her owners.

Roads were primordial, hip-deep in dust in summer. During the wet season, which seemed to be most of the time, mud was deep enough to mire a saddle blanket.

Most early steamboat service along the Cowlitz River fluctuated between poor and indifferent from about 1858 on. Two or three operators attempted to accommodate the trade, but in 1864 the powerful Oregon Steam Navigation Company entered the scene and promptly launched a rate war. Passenger fares between Portland and Monticello (near present-day Longview) dropped to twenty-five cents and freight rates fell correspondingly. Shortly OSN had the market to itself and the quality of service rapidly declined.

To farmers along the Cowlitz the situation became so aggravating that in the late 1870s they persuaded steamboatman Joseph Kellogg to open a new line with promises of profit-making patronage. Associated with Kellogg were his brother and two sons. They built the steamer "Toledo" at Portland and took her to the Cowlitz River. Head of navigation was about two miles above Cowlitz Landing, some thirty-five miles from the mouth. Kellogg, as foresighted as he was ambitious, decided what the place needed was a town. He persuaded some Missourians

"Joseph Kellogg," going about her tasks.

logg had himself a steamboat route with a town at each end. The new community was named Toledo after the stern-wheeler.

The Kellogg Company provided good service. They hauled the mail from Portland along with general store merchandise, farm, mill and logging machinery, dry goods, furniture, building supplies, horses, wagons, and people and their household goods. Downbound, the cargo was mostly farm produce — butter, milk, eggs, live hogs and cattle, hay, potatoes, hops, shingles, lumber, and any other merchandise that had to be moved.

Captains kept a sharp eye for flags along the riverbank which signaled for a pickup. The pilot nosed into the bank for a "mud landing," deckhands threw out the gangplank, loaded the cargo in jig time, and the boat backed off and headed downriver again. There could be a dozen such stops in as many miles.

who had settled at Yaquina Bay, Oregon, to transplant themselves. A town company was formed, a tract of farm land was purchased, a plat was filed, and the enterprising Captain Kel-

"Chester," built at Portland in 1897.

Each boat carried three to six deck-hands who worked for a dollar a day and found.

Pursers and pilots of the "Toledo" and other Kellogg boats often sold farm produce in Portland at prices better than the shipper himself could get. And, like as not, the farmer's wife handed the purser a list of small necessities and notions to be dutifully delivered on the next up trip.

Average round trip passenger fare between Portland and Toledo was two dollars and fifty cents with meals at thirty-five cents. Freight went at three dollars a ton, and small packages brought two bits apiece.

Later Kellogg steamers, such as the "Joseph Kellogg" and "Northwest" offered private staterooms and many a honeymoon started with a trip out to Portland.

Some runs were not without incident. Once a pig, consigned from one Pliny Shepardson to a ranch near Olequa, some miles above Castle Rock, kicked its way out of confinement on the forward deck of the "Chester." The pilot summoned his deckhands to give chase. During the skirmish the pig jumped overboard and swam ashore, the crew in pursuit. The chase ended when Farmer E. R. Huntington's irritated bull joined the party. The pig ran loose until it was captured on a later trip.

Steamboating on the Cowlitz ended in 1918, done in by the highway and the railroad. But by then stern-wheelers had served this important river route for nearly three-quarters of a century, often providing the only link to the outside world and bridging the time between the canoe and the wheel.

Courtesy Oregon Historical Society.

It took a boat with scant draft to safely negotiate the Cowlitz River as far as Toledo. The "Chester" qualified. Loaded, she drew about eighteen inches. With little deadrise, an almost flat bottom, and built full in the bow, "Chester" floated like a scantling.

INGENUITY ON THE UPPER COLUMBIA

Source of the Columbia River is Columbia Lake, just west of the Selkirk Range and only a few miles north of the Montana-British Columbia border. A glance at a map shows one of the Columbia's prime tributaries, the Kootenai, passes a scant mile from Columbia Lake before reaching the mother river many miles to the westward.

Both streams from the early 1880s were served by steamboats, but some of the creations hardly were worthy of the name. The "Duchess" was one. She was assembled at Golden, B. C., of scraps left over from an abandoned Canadian Pacific Railway sawmill. No two boards were of the same thickness and her cabin bore the appearance of an enlarged privy with a penthouse wherein the captain resided with his steering apparatus. Forward motion was provided by an undersized paddle wheel turned by an engine salvaged from a St. Lawrence River ferryboat, originally built in 1840.

The "Duchess" ruled the upper Columbia unrivalled for two years until the even less prepossessing "Clive" arrived to provide competition. The "Clive's" hull was an almost square pile driving scow which also had been abandoned by the railroad. The same sawmill which provided lumber for the "Duchess" was picked over for miscel-

laneous fittings for the "Clive's" engine room. Steam was produced by an upright boiler from a Manitoba plow, and the engine was salvaged from a defunct river tug. The stern-

The remarkable "Duchess."

wheel proved more useful in identifying the boat's stern than in providing propulsion. The "Clive" required twenty-three days to travel the one hundred miles between Golden and Columbia Lake, a portion of the trip being made sideways.

Meantime, a Scots-Austrian expatriate, William Adolph Baillie-Grohman, conceived the scheme of connecting the Kootenai River and Columbia Lake by a canal to merge the two transportation systems into one. Baillie-Grohman formed a syndicate in England, obtained government permission, and commenced work.

By 1889, his canal was completed. It was six thousand, seven hundred feet long and forty-five feet wide, with a wooden lock one hundred by thirty feet. It did, indeed, link two river systems, but the venture was a financial failure. Not until 1893 did the first boat use Baillie-Grohman's canal. This vessel was the "Gwendoline," built that year on the Kootenai, sailed to Canal Flats, and after being partially dismantled, transported on rollers overland to Columbia Lake. Then the "Gwendoline's" owner persuaded the Canadian government to repair the canal locks, and the little craft steamed back through to the Kootenai.

Almost ten years passed before the ditch rendered its second and final service. In that year the "North Star," built at Jennings, Montana, in 1897 for the Kootenai River trade, was purchased by Captain Frank Armstrong with plans to put her on the Columbia as an ore freighter. But there were problems. The canal, so long abandoned, was partially filled in, the old wooden locks were thirty feet shorter than the steamer, and a low bridge with no lift span had been built at Dutch Creek.

Captain Armstrong was not to be deterred by such trifling inconveniences. He worked the "North Star" along the canal as far as the locks. There he tore out the gates, replacing them with sand-filled ore sacks and creating a pond on which the "North Star" floated. Getting up steam, Captain Armstrong had his crew fire off a dynamite charge in the forward wall and the "North Star" dived through to Columbia Lake on the crest. At Dutch Creek, beyond Lake Windermere, the redoubtable Captain met the problem of the bridge with the same ingenuity. He rigged a stiffleg derrick on the "North Star's" bow, hoisted the bridge out of the way, then carefully replaced it after passing through.

After all his labors, Captain Armstrong's plans came to naught. The "North Star" had too much draft for the upper Columbia and could run successfully only during high water. Too, Canadian customs eventually decreed that since no duty had been paid on the vessel she must be laid up. Captain Armstrong complied, but for some years he helped himself to parts and pieces which he transferred to his other boats. Finally, in 1912, the hull was converted into two barges.

WHERE ROLLS THE TUALATIN

A hundred years ago a determined traveler bound from Portland to Forest Grove had a choice of ways to get there. He could travel on horseback or by shank's mare over the Tualatin Hills. In either case he splashed through unbridged streams and marshy bottoms and fought dust or mud depending on the season. Eventually he would reach his destination, fagged out and vowing next time he'd take the steamboat.

That alternative was only slightly less wearing. It did allow for a pleasant boat ride on the steamer "Senator" from Portland to the mouth of Sucker Creek (now Oswego Creek) and an overnight stop at Shade's Hotel in Oswego. Next morning's trip on the "Minnehaha" to the head of the lake was enjoyable, if it wasn't raining.

From lakehead to Colfax Landing on the Tualatin River was about a mile and three quarters by portage railroad. Travelers often traversed the distance afoot just to see if they could beat the engine. They won the contest often as not. At the landing the little stern-wheel steamer "Onward" waited for passengers and freight for flag landings or scheduled stops to Emerick's Landing, sixty miles upstream.

The "Onward's" upbound schedule

A drawing of "Senator."

called for Thursday departures from Colfax Landing; returning, she left Emerick's each Monday at six A.M.

Two predecessors to the "Onward" had been on the Tualatin. First was the side-wheeler "Hoosier," original boat on the Willamette above the Oregon City falls. She began life as a ship's longboat, and was powered by a steam-operated pile driver engine which broke down with distressing frequency. Her time on the Tualatin was brief. The steam-scow "Yamhill," also a side-wheeler, replaced her until the "Onward" took over in 1869. She proved much easier to handle on the narrow, twisting river than had the wider, more clumsy side paddlers.

About this time Oswego was emerging as the region's principal industrial center with incentive supplied by the Oswego Iron Company's productive smelter and supporting mining and charcoal burning enterprises.

When, in March, 1869, the Tualatin River Navigation & Manufacturing Company was incorporated to hasten development of the smelter and its allied activities, the company announced plans to connect Oswego Lake with the Tualatin River by canal. Another canal, with locks, would provide passage at the lake's lower end to the Willamette River, the sponsors proclaimed.

The Lake-Tualatin connection was opened in 1871 but a lengthy period of low water kept the "Onward" from making the first passage until 1873. The second canal never materialized.

For the next twenty years, almost, the Tualatin served as an artery of commerce. Its importance dwindled as improved roads and the extension of rail into the Tualatin Valley cut into the river's freight and passenger trade. Too, the river, always difficult of navigation, seemed never free of snags and sinkers which posed hazards to paddlewheels and wooden hulls. Frequent low water intervals caused delays or complete cessation of schedules.

Finally, in 1895, the Army Corps of Engineers concluded a navigation survey of the Tualatin by pronouncing it unsafe for navigation. Their findings were somewhat after the fact; steamboat service on the river effectively had ceased years before.

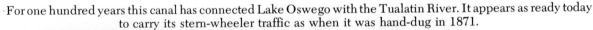

For one hundred years this canal has connected Lake Oswego with the Tualatin River. It appears as ready today to carry its stern-wheeler traffic as when it was hand-dug in 1871.

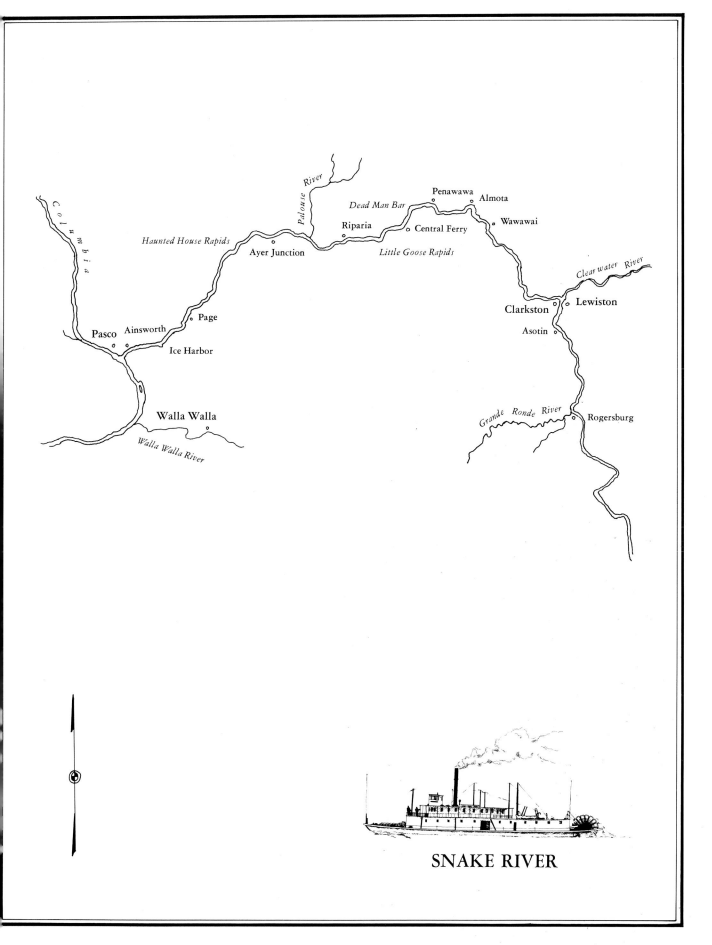

Columbia

Palouse River

Haunted House Rapids

Dead Man Bar

Penawawa   Almota

Riparia

Central Ferry   Wawawai

Ayer Junction

Little Goose Rapids

Clearwater River

Clarkston   Lewiston

Page

Asotin

Pasco   Ainsworth

Ice Harbor

Grande Ronde River   Rogersburg

Walla Walla

Walla Walla River

SNAKE RIVER

"Lewiston," "Spokane," and "J. M. Hannaford" wait out a freeze-up at Lewiston.

"Lewiston" loading at a river bank landing along her Snake River route.

"Imnaha" posed for few pictures. She was built in 1903 at Lewiston to haul ore from the Eureka mine, fifty-five miles upriver. Less than a year and thirteen trips later, through a slight mistake in judgment, she was demolished in Wild Goose Rapids.

Basalt cliffs in the Snake River canyon dwarf "Mountain Gem" at Eureka Bar, fifty-three miles above Lewiston.

A TALE OF TWO LAKES

Courtesy Oregon Historical Society

"Klamath" at Laird's Landing, Lower Klamath Lake, 1907.

The proprietors of the Klamath Lake Navigation Company were perplexed that summer of 1909. Their neat and handsome little two-deck steamer, "Klamath," was in entirely the wrong place. There she was, tied to her dock on Lake Ewauna, the passenger and freight business gone to Hades, and the "Klamath" less than four years old, at that.

"We've got to do *something*," they said to each other. "Can't leave her rot where she is." So they put their minds to the problem and the solution was ingenious indeed.

All Klamath Falls had turned out for the "Klamath's" gala launching. They lined the bank, jostled for viewing space on the wharf, bobbed in rowboats and cheered as the glistening white propeller boat slid stern first off the building ways. The American flag bravely waved from the "Klamath's" stern.

Sherman V. Short and George Woodberry, captain and purser, respectively, of the Columbia River steamer "Dalles City," had come to Klamath Falls to try their luck at inland steamboating. They brought the skilled marine architect J. H. Johnston down from Portland. He was instructed to design a steamer with plenty of freight and passenger space yet with draft slight enough to reach the Lower Lake landings. Johnston obliged. In fact, he sketched out what may well have been the first tunnel type propulsion system on northwest waters. The "Klamath's" propeller was set into a tunnel under the counter which allowed no part of the blades to extend below the keel. The finest workmanship and materi-

als went into the "Klamath." The compound engines, also designed by Johnston, were fabricated under his supervision at Portland. The boiler, obtained from Providence, Rhode Island, could be fueled by wood or coal. From Portland, also, came master builder John G. Sound and his crew of shipwrights.

Small wonder, then, that the "Klamath's" launching occasioned pride and high hopes. On her trial run she clipped off fourteen miles an hour; her engineer bragged she could do twenty without strain.

From the first, the "Klamath" was a success. She made a daily round trip between Klamath Falls and Laird's Landing, fifty miles away at the foot of the lake. From that point travelers could take a stagecoach forty-five miles to the McCloud River Railroad terminus at Bartles and from there to San Francisco. The entire journey took only a day and a half.

But even as the "Klamath" continued her popular service her fate was being written. The very railroad she served as a connecting boat was slowly pushing its tracks northward. The "Klamath's" final trip came on May 27, 1909. The trim little steamer that had survived burst steam pipes, battles with winter ice, damaged propellers (Johnston's invention was not foolproof), and weathered the Navigation Company's receivership had been supplanted by the iron horse.

So her owners pondered the fate of their steamer. That the "Klamath" should be transferred to Upper Klamath Lake seemed reasonable. But short though it was, Link River, which

"Klamath" on her way to new duties on Upper Klamath Lake.

connected the two bodies of water, was unnavigable for the "Klamath." The Klamath Falls *Republican* speculated editorially: "Soundings have recently been taken on the Upper Lake and the reports are that it has been found feasible to operate the "Klamath" to good advantage. In order to move the boat it will be necessary to take it to pieces and rebuild it. The plans of the Klamath Lake Navigation Company will be perfected in the near future and some definite action will then be taken."

For several months the matter lay undecided. In the end, the answer was simple, though ironic. As an old-timer recalls: "A (dredge) cut was made from Lake Ewauna through the tules to the railroad fill about where the Big Lakes Mill is now. A spur track was built to it. The boat was raised onto timbers and two flat cars run under it, where it was made solid by blocking, and hauled to the Upper Lake and unloaded the same way."

The irony was that the same railroad which had ended the first phase of the "Klamath's" career was instrumental in extending the steamer's life for a few more years.

For awhile the "Klamath" ran as an excursion boat to the Crater Lake stage line landing on Crystal Creek. In 1911, she was converted to an oil burner and about the same time she was sold to the Pelican Bay Lumber Co. as a raft towing and logging camp supply boat.

In the few years remaining to her the once-handsome "Klamath" fell on hard times. Finally, worn out and forgotten by the fickle applauders at her launching, she was tied to the bank in the Pelican Bay log cut to ignominiously weather to pieces.

QUEEN OF COEUR d'ALENE

The planning committee had done its job well and Coeur d'Alene was going to have a Fourth of July observance the people would not soon forget. The orators would be in strong voice and full of ringing platitudes; the band had practiced until its members could conclude most of the martial airs at approximately the same time; there would be plenty to eat, with a ballgame and footraces for the youngsters and energetic adults. Of course, there would be fireworks. "But what should

we do as climax?" the committee asked each other. "Something grand to top it off is what we need."

Then someone remembered that old steamboat rotting away down on the waterfront, and they had their answer.

So it happened that as darkness fell on that July 4th in 1927 the crowds "oh'd" and "ah'd" and cheered as the flames crackled and the waters of Lake Coeur d'Alene reflected back the finish of the "Georgie Oakes."

The Northern Pacific Railway built

"Georgie Oakes," prior to rebuilding in 1908.

the big stern-wheeler in 1890 and named her after a daughter of the line's president. Her purpose at first was to carry any conceivable kind of freight and all the passengers she could cram aboard down-lake to the Coeur d'Alene Mountain gold mines and to haul sacked ore back. From the steamer dock at the village of Coeur d'Alene, the NP delivered the ore to smelters at Spokane.

The "Georgie Oakes" could handle a hundred tons of ore (her predecessor had half the capacity) and as many as five hundred passengers a trip and do it at a respectable eighteen miles an hour.

She served this trade for almost ten years until the mining boom dwindled and rail tracks penetrated the back country. But even as the gold and silver seekers moved out, the loggers moved in, bringing new work for the "Georgie Oakes" to do. She plugged away for the Northern Pacific until in 1908 she was declared unsafe and was laid up. The Red Collar Line, engaged in a hot rivalry for traffic with the White Star Navigation Company, bought the old boat. A few months and about ten thousand dollars later the "Georgie Oakes" was back in service, practically rebuilt but as speedy and capacious as before.

Under command of profane, colorful Captain Eli Laird, the "Georgie Oakes" chuffed up and down the lake six days a week on her assigned freight and passenger duties. But on Sunday she was transformed. The residents of Spokane and surrounding communities had discovered the beauties of Lake Coeur d'Alene and its tributary river, the "shadowy St. Joe." Excursion trains disgorged eager sightseers from a dozen Inland Empire cities, and most of them headed for the "Georgie Oakes." "Cap" Laird was an attraction, with his wealth of anecdotes, and so were the far-famed fish feeds of "Tex" Arner, lord and master of the "Georgie Oakes'" galley.

So, as often happens though no one can for certain say why, the "Georgie Oakes" became a part of the life and legend of the region. Until 1917 she played her dual role — ordinary work-boat from Monday to Saturday, magic carpet on Sunday. But finally business began to drop off under the pressure of rival boats and as the automobile presented new diversions for the weekend excursionists.

The "Georgie Oakes" kept trying for a few years more, running occasionally until 1920, but at last she was tied up for good. Perhaps it was right that she ended as she did, sent to glory in a well-meant patriotic gesture. But there must have been some who watched the burning with a damp eye and sighed with the memories of green hills and blue lake and white water cascading from a churning paddlewheel.

"White Horse" climbing Five Finger Rapids on the the Yukon River. Captain George M. Shaver is at the wheel.

PERILOUS PASSAGES

Until the Cascade Locks were opened in 1873 and the Celilo Canal in 1915, the Columbia River was, like Gaul, divided into three parts. The Lower, Middle and Upper Rivers effectively were separated by almost impassible barriers, steep falls at Tumwater, ten miles above The Dalles, and at the Cascades, some forty miles below. Boats serving each part exchanged cargo and passengers at portages. In the beginning, these were trails. Mule-pulled carts running on wooden tracks followed and finally these gave way to iron rails and steam engines.

Occasionally, boats by accident or by intent went through the white water. The "Venture" didn't really mean to, back in 1858, on her maiden voyage. As soon as she was launched, forty passengers clambered aboard for the trial trip. Before the engineer got up enough steam the captain ordered the lines cast off. The "Venture," caught by the current, skyrocketed through the Cascades stern first. She made it nicely but impaled herself on a rock at the foot of the chute where she sat until the next high water floated her off. The only casualty was one panic-stricken passenger who jumped overboard in mid-descent and drowned.

After the "Venture" had proved it could be done, other boats tried the passage. It was the only way to get a vessel from the middle to the lower river and careful skippers waited until the top of high water. During the spring freshet of 1881, a clutch of them sailed down, among them the "Mountain

Steamer "Spencer."

"Cascades" dropping across Cascade Rapids with seven hundred fifty tons of wheat in 1934.

Queen." Spectators watched the show from passenger cars on the portage railroad. They scarcely got their money's worth for they were three hundred yards back by the time the "Queen" reached the lower end, even though her time had been a relatively slow eleven minutes.

Worse than the Cascades, though shorter, were the series of rapids and chutes at Celilo with the grandaddy of the lot, Tumwater Falls, at the top. A number of craft, beginning with the "Umatilla," negotiated this run. The most noteworthy trip was that of the "Harvest Queen," commanded by Captain James Troup. On her first pitch she lost both rudders and part of the stern wheel. Control gone, she slewed into a boulder and punctured her hull, then swerved across the channel into a reef and smashed away part of the bow. The anchor was dropped; it was torn away by the force of the current. Only a kedge saved the "Queen" and she worked her way to shore for repairs. A week later, Captain Troup completed the run without further incident.

"Hassalo" at The Dalles wharfboat. With the Columbia impassable above The Dalles, freight and passengers transferred to the portage railroad for the thirteen mile trip above Celilo Falls.

CAPTAIN WINSLOW'S FABULOUS
FLYING MACHINE

Captain Winslow's Fabulous Flying Machine.

The career of Captain Stewart V. Winslow, one of the most respected steamboat captains, reached across sixty years, from 1889 as a deckhand on Snake River stern-wheelers until 1949 when he retired from the Columbia River Pilots Association. Only once did Captain Winslow desert his element in a diversion that might have cost his life and did focus nationwide attention on Lewiston, Idaho. It came to pass in 1904. Captain Winslow for years had

been fascinated by the flight of pigeons, watching their landings and takeoffs and soaring glides as he leaned out his pilot house window. And he absorbed all he could read about the experiments with aircraft then being made.

With the Wright brothers' first powered flight December 17, 1903, Captain Winslow felt his time had come. From duties as first officer on the steamer "Spokane" he stole all the time he could spare while the boat was tied up at the Lewiston landing. With the help of interested crew members, Captain Winslow built a heavier-than-air craft. *The Lewiston Tribune*, in its July 30, 1904, edition, described the machine. "The body . . . consists of two planes being attached one above the other. The planes are about four feet wide and the upper one is seventeen and one half feet long. The lower plane is fourteen feet in length and to this is attached a horizontal sheet rudder . . . that can be raised and lowered at will to regulate the ascent or descent. In the rear is a fin rudder that preserves the equilibrium . . . and guides its flight. Extending from the frame . . . are two wings measuring twenty-four feet from tip to tip, and by bamboo stays a large area of canvas is gained by each wing." Motive power was a bicycle, propelled by the Captain himself.

Thus, a scant six months after the Wright brothers' flight, Captain Winslow's aircraft was poised at the top of a seven hundred foot bluff overlooking the Snake. A three hundred foot plank track led down the slope to the bluff's edge. It was the Captain's intention to gain enough speed to become airborne and to soar safely across the river toward fame. Just as the machine "was filling and lifting from the ground" it struck a rock, punctured a tire and slewed off the track. Captain Winslow, bruised and frustrated, dragged the broken pieces to a warehouse, intending to make repairs and try again.

He never got around to it. Almost thirty years later, the Army sent its judge advocate general to Lewiston to locate the wreckage. The Captain had patented his creation, and advancements in aircraft design brought specters of infringement to the War Department. But, by then, the evidence was gone and with it also went hopes of the Smithsonian Institution, which wished to obtain the plane for enshrinement among its aeronautical exhibits.

TO THE HEAD OF NAVIGATION

A natural outgrowth of the development of steamboat transportation on the waters of the Columbia-Willamette-Snake river system was a multitude of transportation companies. Some were endowed with larger portions of confidence and profit motive than of business acumen. A number blossomed in an attempt to break the stranglehold of the monopolistic Oregon Steam Navigation Company — and died quickly under pressures applied by this monolith.

Other ventures were formed, sometimes shortly merging with competitors, sometimes remaining independent, to provide transportation services on tributary streams where the trade was not profitable enough to attract the high and mighty O.S.N.

A few corporations active during the 1860s and 1870s were the Willamette River Transportation Co., Vancouver Steamboat Co., Tualatin River Navigation & Transportation Co., Cowlitz Steam Navigation Co., Willamette

"Columbia" retired in 1914 when the railroad replaced her. At Wenatchee she lands sacked wheat from upriver points to the dock for transfer to waiting box cars.

"Lucea Mason" was built at St. Helens, Oregon, in 1883 and was owned by Farmers' Transportation Company. L. P. Hosford is the man with the black beard standing on the upper deck.

Freighting Co., People's Transportation Co., Willamette Transportation & Lock Co., Columbia Transportation Co., and Farmer's Transportation Co.

One of the more successful and longer-lived ventures was the Lewis & Lake River Transportation Co., founded in 1876 by farmers living along those streams. Their purpose was to provide a sure and economical route to the Portland market.

What better way than to create and control it themselves? Eventually the company operated a substantial fleet, acquiring some boats from less well-managed rivals, building others.

Among the stern-wheelers that flew the flag of the Lewis River Co. (as it came to be known were the "Hydra," "Swallow," "Latona," "Lucea Mason," "Charm," "Dewdrop," "Columbia," and "La Center." For eighteen years, longer than any other steamboatman on the run, Captain W. G. Weir commanded boats of the company.

There were other Weirs who learned their steamboating on the Lewis river run, among them Captain Cassius, father, and Captain Earl, son. The former got into business by trading the family farm near La Center, Washington, for a steamboat and soliciting passengers and freight. One of Captain Cassius' proudest claims was that he was the first to pilot a steamboat to a point above the present site of Ariel Dam.

None of the Lewis River Company fleet was noted for its speed or fancy accommodations. They simply were utility or jobbing boats of shallow draft,

a hundred feet or less in length, capable of carrying about one hundred and twenty-five tons of freight.

The Lewis, like many another of the smaller rivers, was perilous to navigate. Sunken logs, unmarked rocks, and similar underwater hazards occasionally brought the boats to grief. When this happened, they were patiently raised, patched, and returned to service.

The fleet made money for its owners. It performed a vital service until paved roads and speedier trucks stilled the throaty whistles and softly chuffing exhausts. Only then did one era give way to another, leaving only lingering memories of a slower-paced time.

"Mascot," prime example of a jobbing boat, mostly served the Lewis River trade.

Oregon City Transportation Co., the "Yellow Stack Line," operated "Latona" (ex-"McMinnville" of 1899) as a day boat.

The "Yellow Stack Line" ended all its boat names in "-ona." "Grahamona" was named after the Graham family, owners of the line. As "Northwestern," she was sold in 1939 for service on Alaska's Kuskokwim River.

With a GAR outing party aboard, "Grahamona" wedges her way through Willamette Falls locks.

BELIEVE IT OR NOT . . .

"The Mountain Queen" (renamed the Sehome) built on the Columbia River in 1877, was first a stern-wheeler, then a side-wheeler — and finally became a propeller ship."
    — Ripley's Believe It or Not, 13th Series

This titillating item about the "Mountain Queen" is true enough, but the researchers could have added a last line with enough touch of the unusual to appeal to Ripley's readers.

Oregon Steam Navigation Company rushed the "Mountain Queen" off the ways in the spring of 1877 to replace the "Daisy Ainsworth," which had struck a rock in a fog at Upper Cascades the winter before. (Coincidentally, the very day the "Queen" was launched, the wreckage of the "Ainsworth" slipped off the rocks and drifted over

"Mountain Queen" in 1877.

the Cascades to final destruction.) The "Queen" was given the "Ainsworth's" engines in a hull one hundred and seventy-six feet long, thirty two feet wide and seven feet six inches deep. She served on the middle river until Captain James W. Troup took her over the Cascades in July, 1882. For the next seven years, under as many masters, the "Queen" ran on the Astoria and Cascades routes.

At Portland in 1889 the "Queen" was rebuilt as a side-wheeler, lengthened by sixteen feet, renamed the "Sehome" and sent by the Oregon Railway and Navigation Company, successors to O.S.N., to Puget Sound. She operated in freight and passenger service between Tacoma and Seattle, Vancouver, B.C., and Whatcom until her owners pulled out of Puget Sound steamboating and sent the "Sehome" and others of their fleet into layup or sale.

For several years the "Sehome" moldered at the Tacoma seawall, picking up an occasional charter for the Northern Pacific Railway. Her revival came in 1900 when she was overhauled and placed on the Tacoma-Whatcom run. Then, in 1902, the Pacific Coast Steamship Company, mainly deep-sea operators, entered the Puget Sound steamboat business, buying the "Sehome" and the "State of Washington" for fifty thousand dollars and placing them on their Seattle-Bellingham Bay route.

A few years later, Monticello Steamship Company, largest operators on San Francisco Bay with a fleet of ferries, passenger boats, and coastwise ocean steamers, obtained the venerable "Sehome" and took her south. Under this ownership she underwent in 1914 yet another metamorphosis, losing her paddlewheels and emerging as a propeller boat.

Back and forth across the Bay she plodded, wearing her age well. Through the years of the first World War the "Sehome" carried passengers and freight, setting no records, engaging in no theatrics. In 1918, at the age of forty-one, Fate in the form of the coastal steamer "General Frisbie" overtook the twice-transformed old lady.

The "Sehome" was on one of her regular crossings, plugging along on schedule and on route, when the faster, bigger "General Frisbie," on a converging course, rammed and sank her. And here is where Ripley's writers could have added the wry final note — the Monticello Steamship Company also owned the "General Frisbie."

THE LARGEST THINGS AFLOAT

Across the slowly surging Columbia River bar into the open ocean, moving ponderously at the end of a quarter-mile towing cable as the tug found sea-room and steadied down on course, for more than twenty years there passed the most unusual products of one man's ingenuity.

These were the famed "cigar" rafts, six million and more board feet of timber bound into a solid mass by ships' anchor chains. Like an iceberg

A completed "cigar" raft, ready to be taken out by its steamer.

they floated, drawing twenty feet of water with only a scant seven feet of freeboard. They were unwieldy and cantankerous to tow. But they were the most economical way of moving large amounts of high-value Pacific

completed to San Francisco. Although similar tries met with various success in later years, it remained for a Norwegian immigrant named Simon Bergerson to perfect the scheme.

Simon's parents first settled in the

All available hands, including the cook, gather for their picture, snapped from an ocean-going log raft downbound to Astoria to meet a deep-water tug.

Northwest timber to the hungry southern California market. During the boom as many as five of these gigantic rafts left the river each year.

The first attempt to take a raft from the Columbia to California was made in 1894. Improperly fastened, it broke up in a gale, scattering giant Douglas fir logs over hundreds of square miles of ocean, a lethal menace to navigation. The next year a successful tow was

Wisconsin lumber country where the family name was Anglicized to Benson. By 1879, young Benson was operating a logging show in Columbia County, Oregon. He is credited with introducing steam donkey-engine and rail equipment into the Northwest woods. He prospered to become a philanthropist, hotel builder and good roads enthusiast. But one of his enduring monuments is the log raft he devised.

On a pleasant Sunday, the crew assembles for their picture at a Benson "cigar" raft boom.

His first, built in 1906, was assembled in a cradle that supported the logs as they were tightly bound into a cigar-shaped raft. When the cradle was released the raft floated free. Pushed by stern-wheelers to Astoria, it was turned over there to powerful ocean steam tugs like the "Humaconna" and "Roosevelt" for the long tow to San Diego. For their day, Benson log rafts were the largest man-made objects afloat.

Each year thereafter, until the mid-30s when the depression brought an end to the California building boom, "cigar" rafts went south. Most contained about six million board feet of logs with deckloads of one hundred thousand board feet of lumber and piling. They were up to nine hundred feet long by fifty-four feet wide and drew thirty-six feet. So well-built were Benson's rafts that of the one hundred or more he dispatched, only two or three broke up, and parts of these were salvaged.

A BAD DAY FOR THE "LEWISTON"

Some days just shouldn't start. And that's probably how Captain E. E. Davis of the steamer "Lewiston" began to fell pretty early on February 29, 1940. He and his crew already had waited for almost a month for enough high water on the Snake River to safely navigate the one hundred and forty miles from Lewiston to the Columbia and then on down to Portland. The Union Pacific Co., owners of the "Lewiston," had sold her to Western Transportation Co., and Captain Davis was to deliver her to the new owners.

Hundreds lined the river bank as the "Lewiston" prepared to sail from her dock just upstream from the bridge. A reporter aboard recounts the next events.

"At 8:55 a.m. lines were cast off and the "Lewiston's" deep-throated whistle sounded three blasts, the signal for opening the lift span of the bridge.

"Nothing happened, and the steamer stood idling at the bank, its paddle wheel turning slowly. Five minutes of patient waiting and Captain Davis again sounded the signal. This time, screaming sirens on the bridge wailed in response as the lift span was slowly raised by its electric motors.

"Puffing great clouds of white smoke against an overcast sky, the veteran steamer moved slowly into the stream and was probably a third of the way into the main channel when its power failed.

"Old-time rivermen, sensing the danger when the huge paddle wheel stopped churning, anxiously watched as the current whipped the steamer toward the bridge. But few among the spectators were aware of the accident and hundreds who lined the bridge railings cheered as the steamer swiftly floated through the narrow gap and soon was out of sight around the bend."

The "Lewiston" drifted ashore a quarter-mile below where it was found an engine valve had frozen. Repairs were made and she got underway at eleven-thirty A.M., only to have the same valve freeze once more while Captain Davis was turning her head downstream. Back to shore she went. The valve was unstuck, but less than seven miles farther, a broken push-rod halted her and an aggravated Captain Davis tied to the bank for the night.

The push-rod was repaired at a Lewiston welding shop, replaced the next morning, and the lines were hesitantly cast off. Before eight-thirty, a clogged oil burner feed line forced another engine shut-down. This was quickly corrected, and by eleven thirty-five the "Lewiston" had maneuvered to the head of Granite Point rapids. At this crucial moment the engines gave a groaning shudder, the chief

For most of her life a railroad boat, "Lewiston" handled passengers and freight on the lower Snake between Asotin and Riparia for the Union Pacific.

From "Lewiston" of 1923 emerged "Barry K," for a few years a lower Columbia towboat before transferring to the Tanana and Yukon rivers for the Alaska Railroad.

engineer rang them down, and for three miles she drifted powerless as the captain fought the wheel and the passengers prayed. Safely tied again to the bank, she lay there two days for more repairs, this time to the rocker arm.

On Monday morning, three days and twenty-eight miles from home, her benumbed crew untied the mooring lines once again. Finally the "Lewiston" decided to cooperate, and the voyage to Portland, where she arrived Wednesday, proceeded without incident.

A month later she had lost her old name and had become the towboat "Barry K." In 1943 the Army took her over and she joined the fleet of stern-wheelers operated by the Alaska Railroad on the Yukon and Tanana rivers. There she ended her days as she had begun them, a railroad boat.

In January, 1965, Captain E. E. Davis retired from his position as a Columbia River pilot since 1949, ending a forty seven year career. He had started work on the stern-wheeler "F. B. Jones" as a deckhand in 1918. He earned his mate's papers in 1921, his master's license in 1927, and was captain of the Astoria ferry, "M. R. Chessman," when it was placed in service in April, 1948.

"Dalles City" entering Cascade Locks.

WORK HORSES OF THE COLUMBIA

The fast and fancy "palace boats" got most of the publicity and the bulk of the passenger trade during the golden days of Columbia River steamboating. But dozens of less glamorous work horses did their unheralded daily chores of hauling freight and passengers to scores of landings along hundreds of miles of the river and its tributaries.

Such a one was the "Dalles City," undistinguished as to looks and speed, yet eminently capable of keeping schedules and earning money for her

"Regulator" (1891) was instrumental in reviving a dwindling Columbia River steamboat trade during the nineties. Her owners, Dalles, Portland & Astoria Navigation Co., became known as "The Regulator Line."

"Charles R. Spencer" makes an informal landing at Hood River while passengers pose and deckhands hustle under the purser's watchful eye.

the delights of the metropolis, mingled in the pleasant main cabin with drummers bound for Walla Walla and Burns and Lewiston, they were doing nothing less than today's casual travelers. The mode and tempo of transportation only are different.

Occasionally, excitement spiced the trip, as when the "Hassalo" got herself stuck on a rock and couldn't work off. The "Dalles City" came by and took her passengers, dropping the deck fares off at Vancouver, and carrying the first class ticket holders on to Portland.

Or when the irresistible urge to race descended simultaneously on three captains. The "Dalles City," "Charles R. Spencer," and "Telegraph" pulled away from their Portland berths at the same time, and each captain at once ordered full speed ahead on his engines.

Tightly bunched, the stern-wheelers plowed down the harbor, their bow waves piling up against the wharves lining the narrow channel. The rolling swell smashed into the British steamer, "Agincourt." She rolled sharply over and back, snapping her stern hawser. The gangway pulled away from the dock and dropped back, splintered; the bridge railing crumpled against the dock house. The furious skipper stormed ashore and into the courthouse, where three chastened captains later appeared to post fifty dollars bail apiece on charges of having violated the city's speed limits.

owners. She was built in Portland in 1891 for a new transportation line, The Dalles, Portland and Astoria Navigation Co., which at once placed her and the "Regulator" in service on the Portland-The Dalles run. Of four hundred and two tons burden and one hundred and forty-two feet in length, the "Dalles City" plugged away at her job carrying sacks of grain, barrels of apples, bolts of yard goods, and the assorted merchandise required by the emporiums of the river towns at which she called.

And, if central Oregon farmers and their families, headed back home from

IT WAS ALL IN THE FAMILY

Shoalwater Bay, in Pacific County's southwestern corner, first saw "Governor Newell" in 1883, but the visit was brief. A couple of years later she transferred to the Columbia, becoming the command of Captain Minnie Hill, first licensed female steamboat captain in the western U.S.A.

A couple of generations ago it was common to say the average boy's highest ambition was to become either a fireman or locomotive engineer. A goodly number, however, succumbed to the lure of surging pitman rods and spray-splashed paddle wheels and went steamboating. There were plenty of opportunities on the waters of the Columbia River and Puget Sound.

Sons followed fathers; cousins, uncles, in-laws were in engine room or pilot house.

Captain James H. Whitcomb and his five boys formed the largest early family of steamboatmen in the Pacific Northwest. Captain James started the family trade in 1858. Until well after the turn of the century his sons commanded steamers on Gray's Harbor, Shoalwater Bay, and the Columbia River.

In the equally-well known Buchanan family were Captain William J., who started steamboating on the Ohio and continued on the Columbia after arriving in Oregon in 1869, his brother Captain Isaac, son Captain William S., and nephew Frank J. The family venture was centered on the Willamette and Columbia Rivers.

Active during the same period were the brothers John, George, and Charles Gore, transplants from Michigan. John was a mate at sixteen, a captain while still in his teens. George, cabin boy at fourteen, mate at seventeen and master a few years later, piloted several boats on which brother Charles was engineer.

The list runs on — Troups, Scotts, Grays, Shavers, Hoyts and others all contributing their share to the region's steamboat history and lore.

But the most unusual team of all was Captain Charles O. Hill and his wife Minnie. In 1889, Captain Charles purchased the stern-wheel steamer, "Governor Newell," which had operated with moderate fortune on Shoalwater Bay and the lower Columbia. His

Courtesy Oregon Historical Society

Captain Minnie Hill.

young wife Minnie, who in 1886 enjoyed the distinction of becoming the first licensed female steamboat captain west of the Mississippi, at once took command and operated the vessel with remarkable success for several years. Most of the time Captain Charles ran as her engineer. Captain Minnie was twenty-three when she was licensed, twenty-six when she became master (or mistress) of the "Governor Newell."

"JOHN DAY," LANDLOCKED QUEEN

In every boy's breast beats the pulse of adventure. Some early realize their dream and become brave firemen or policemen, ship captains, airplane pilots, or big game hunters. For others, as for Charlie Clarno, it takes a little longer to get there. Charlie was thirty-two when his dream was fulfilled at the John Day River hamlet named after his homesteading family one hundred and nine miles south of the Columbia River in Oregon's desolate interior.

Charlie was about five years old when his folks, first settlers on the river, reached John Day country. Although the boy grew up with cattle and horses, the lure of the river never was far from him. How strong it was is told in a 1938 story from Portland's Oregon Journal:

"In 1895, Charlie Clarno . . . launched the "John Day Queen," the only steamer ever to operate on the John Day River. . . .

"As a boy, Charlie Clarno had experimented with building small boats . . . including the ferry he operated at the Clarno post office. . . . After he reached his majority he had saved enough money to buy a boiler, lumber and equipment to set about building a miniature stern-wheeler patterned after the larger boats operating on the Columbia River. It was approximately forty feet long, ten feet high and ten feet wide. The pilot house was three feet high and three feet wide, just wide enough for Charlie's head and shoulders. He stood on a platform to operate the steering helm."

Charlie loved to take friends and neighbors the dozen navigable miles above and below Clarno, "demonstrating his ability as both captain and engineer." Passengers often were required to cut wood along the bank to fire the boiler, but no one objected. In those days of scant community entertainment, ranch families would come a hundred miles to ride on the "John Day Queen" or to enjoy moonlight dance cruises. Charlie played the banjo, apparently running the boat at the same time, and his sister Laura played the organ. There usually was a fiddler handy to round out the music.

The Journal account continues: "The John Day Queen" was used for rescue purposes during high water and . . . as a passenger ferry at Clarno until the bridge was built in 1897." Because the river could be forded at low water, Charlie would warn greenhorns of imaginary quicksand to extract a dollar to ferry them safely across. Stage drivers and natives wouldn't bite.

Charlie sold his farm with the coming of the bridge and moved to Portland. But a few years later he was back, planning to bring the "Queen" down to the metropolis and run her as an excursion boat. At Clarno, the John Day is one thousand, two hundred and ninety feet above sea level. It drops ten feet in the four miles below town, then in the next mile it plunges forty feet lower over a series of rapids. Charlie's plan was folly and, though he tried the run in spring high water, the "Queen" was holed and sunk on the first rapid.

An orchardist at The Dalles bought the wreck to salvage the boiler for his pumping plant. He got it out of the river and hauled as far as Shaniko where it rusted away in a wool warehouse. Charlie, the dream ended and the fun over, went back to Portland.

"John Day Queen."

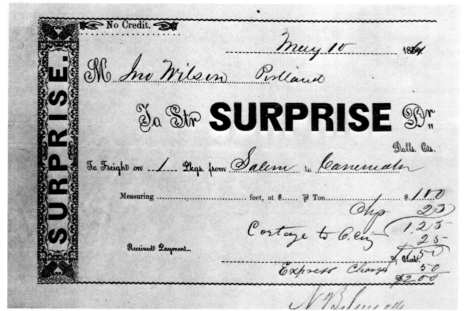

1861 freight bill for steamer "Surprise."

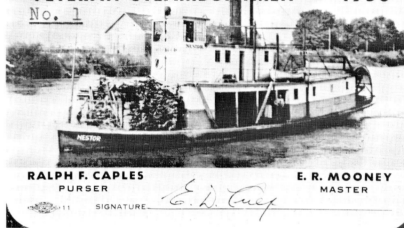

RALPH F. CAPLES
PURSER

E. R. MOONEY
MASTER

Membership card in the Veteran Steamboatmen's Association, proudly carried by "river rats."

A Master's license enabling a Mr. Pillsbury to command a steamboat in 1884.

This pass allowed H. Trinwith to ride the boats of the Oregon City Transportation Company.

HOW TO CORNER THE MARKET

When the Oregon Steam Navigation Company's officers undertook to extend their monopoly over the transportation system of the Pacific Northwest, their efforts were nothing if not direct and total. During the period of O.S.N.'s domination, 1860 to 1879, all major steamboat routes, stage lines, portages, and railroads at one time or another came under the com-

Crack O. S. N. steamer on the Celilo-Lewiston run was "Yakima," built in 1864 and wrecked at John Day Rapids in 1875. She was fast and commodious, with excellent freight capacity.

"Mary Moody" on Lake Pend d'Oreille.

pany's control. Rivals were purchased or were forced out in disastrous rate wars. A few competitors were tolerated because they were content to serve minor tributaries that the O.S.N. disdained, or were operated on a profit margin slim enough to be unattractive.

In fairness it must be noted that O.S.N. service was excellent. The boats ran as advertised. Mostly, they were comfortable and rapid, and the meals and beds were good. Passenger and freight tariffs were high, except during a rate battle, but after all the company was out to make a profit. Besides, a traveler had little choice except to walk or fork a horse and a shipper's only alternatives were pack train or wagon.

The O.S.N. was alert to every opportunity to extend its holdings and when the Montana gold rush commenced in the mid-1860s, it moved.

The route from Portland to the Missoula mining region put to the test the O.S.N.'s service, and no less it tested the miner bound for the diggings. He left Portland by boat, took the rail portage at Cascade Locks, then was carried by another boat to The Dalles where he portaged around Celilo Falls. A third steamboat took him to a Snake River landing from whence he faced a bone-bruising stage ride to the head of Lake Pend d'Oreille.

During yet another steamboat trip across the lake and up Clarke's Fork River to Cabinet Rapids the traveler could recuperate and prepare for further travail. After a short stage ride he boarded the steamer, "Cabinet," for the run to Thompson's Falls. Above this obstruction waited the "Missoula," last link in this seemingly endless transportation chain, to convey the weary argonaut a few miles farther to the mouth of the Jocko River. Here the O.S.N.'s obligations ended; it had run out of rivers. At that point the sufferer was on his own, yet a hundred miles from the Missoula mining region.

His fare from Wallula, roughly the mid-way point, had been thirty-two dollars and fifty cents. Freight moved at seven cents a pound, which sounds more palatable than one hundred and forty dollars a ton, but considering the number of times the merchandise had been handled the price probably was a bargain.

On the Pend d'Oreille-Jocko route, the O.S.N. preferred to operate through a subsidiary, the Oregon & Montana Transportation Company. First boat the new firm put into service was the "Mary Moody," built to operate on Lake Pend d'Oreille. She was constructed in four months time from lumber whipsawed at the site. Her engines came from the "Express" of 1854, second stern-wheeler in the Pacific Northwest. They had arrived by wagon from the Snake River whence they had been transported by steamer from Portland. The "Mary Moody" made her first trip in May, 1867, a voyage of some seventy miles across the lake and up Clarke's Fork to the foot of Cabinet Rapids.

Concerning the opening of this three-boat, two portage route, a writer for *Harper's Monthly* had this fulsome observation:

"This plan in operation, the northwestern portion of Montana, surpassingly rich in agricultural facilities, and faraway the most beautiful portion of the territory, the scenery of it blending all the sterner and loftier with all the gentler features of Switzerland and the Tyrol, will be pierced and opened from the Pacific and a future of prosperous activity secured for it, which no one can presume at this moment to shadow forth, much less to estimate."

His crystal ball was murky. By early 1870 the bloom was off the rose and business dropped sharply. The "Cabinet" and "Missoula" were brought down through Hero Rapids to the head of Cabinet Canyon in a spine-chilling white-water run in June of that year. A few weeks later, after the water dropped, the two steamers were taken on to Lake Pend d'Oreille.

Though a small amount of custom developed on the lake, the three stern-wheelers lay idle most of the time until 1876. Then the O.S.N. dismantled them and hauled their machinery overland to Texas Ferry on the Snake and back down the Columbia to Portland.

On balance, the venture had proven unprofitable. But in a couple of ways it did succeed; it reaffirmed O.S.N. domination of the region's transportation, and it successfully discouraged any rivals from poaching on the company's preserve.

JINX OF THE "OCKLAHAMA"

"Ocklahama" assists a loaded grain ship downstream past the old Portland gas works. A steam tug, almost obscured by the stern-wheeler's upper works, lends a hand.

It was to be expected that a Columbia River stern-wheeler would be involved during her career in a number of groundings, puncturings, breakdowns, and assorted mishaps. Barring a fire or boiler explosion severe enough to cause extensive rebuilding or total destruction the vessel usually would be back in service a few weeks later.

Under stress of competition, captains might overlook a few precautionary safety measures. Unmarked rocks, shifting channels, and unexpected snags took their toll. Little attention was paid to the more minor adversities. These were regarded as a routine part of steamboating.

When the "Ocklahama" was involved in misfortune it was in the grand style. And she didn't even have to be in the vicinity. Take the case of the "Clan Mackenzie." The "Ocklahama" had towed the British square rigger from Astoria as far as Kalama, then had dropped her in the channel while the stern-wheeler ran into shore to wood up. The "Clan Mackenzie" was swinging idly on the hook when the steamship "Oregon," heavily loaded and bound to sea, came ripping down the channel. She struck the "Clan Mackenzie" between stem and cathead on the port bow. When the "Ocklahama" came paddling back to pick up her tow, all she found was several masts sticking up out of the river.

"Ocklahama," a Western Transportation Co. steamer once owned by the Port of Portland, waits for the Morrison Street bridge draw.

Earlier the "Ocklahama" herself had been involved in a pair of accidents. In 1886 she was alongside the bark "Alliance" at a Portland dock preparing to move the ship out into the stream. Suddenly the "Alliance" heeled over atop the "Ocklahama," smashing pilot house, hogchains, and smokestack, and slightly injuring Captain H. A. Emken at the wheel. The stern-wheeler supported the dead weight of the "Alliance" until her shifted cargo was moved and the bark could stand alone. Then the "Ocklahama" limped off for repairs.

Shortly afterward, one of the steamer's tows sank at an Astoria wharf,

"Ocklahama" between two windships.

causing thirty thousand dollars damage to the other craft. Claims against the "Ocklahama" tied her up for a time, but she finally was released on bond and returned to work.

The greatest tragedy to involve the "Ocklahama" occurred in 1892, also at Astoria, where she had towed the barge "Columbia," carrying five hundred and fifty tons of wheat. While swinging into the wharf the barge struck with such force that it was holed and began to take water. Captain Marshall Short maneuvered into the shallows. The "Ocklahama" hooked up to pump out the barge, and Captain Short and four others went below to construct a

bulkhead at the damage point. They had almost finished when the barge heeled over and sank. Three escaped, but shifting grain trapped Captain Short and deckhand John Peterson, drowning both.

Some years passed before the "Ocklahama's" jinx walked again. The year was 1913, and she was towing the German four-masted bark, "Thielbek," on the lower Columbia. The Norwegian steamer, "Thode Fagelund," outward bound with lumber, collided with the bark with such force that the two vessels could not be pried apart for several hours.

The remainder of the "Ocklahama's"

career was less eventful. In 1916, she was purchased from her then owners, The Port of Portland Commission, by Western Transportation Company, running for that firm until her retirement in 1930.

The "Ocklahama" had been active since 1875, undergoing a two-year layup and rebuilding between 1894 and 1897. To offset her dismal chronicle of misfortune, she had two records to her credit: she was built as the first stern-wheeler on the river solely for towing purposes, and in her lifetime, towed more ships than any other boat on the Columbia.

"Ocklahama" with festive decor.

FASTEST PASSAGE

Every once in a while, among the hundreds of steamboats built for the waters of the Pacific Northwest, there came one that proved memorable. Such was the elegant "R. R. Thompson." She was built at The Dalles in 1878 for the Oregon Steam Navigation Company's middle river service. Her connecting boats were the "Wide West," between Portland and the Cascades, and the "John Gates" and "Spokane" from Celilo upriver.

The "Thompson" was a big boat for her day. Her two hundred and fifteen foot length and thirty-eight foot beam allowed for spacious passenger accom-modations with ample room for freight. Passenger spaces were nicely fitted out and the ladies' cabin boasted carpets, plush settees, and polished panelled walls. The "Thompson" was not a fast boat. Rather, she deliberately was built for comfort and truly qualified for such overblown adjectives as "palace boat" and "finest cuisine afloat," whipped up by enthusiastic passenger agents of the day.

For four years her popularity remained undiminished on the middle river, until completion of the south bank railroad from Portland eastward spelled doom for the steamboat fleet.

For ten years "Wide West" was flagship of the O.S.N. fleet. When retired, she gave over her upper works and engines to emerge as the side-wheeler "T. J. Potter."

One by one, the stern-wheelers were brought down over the Cascades.

The "R. R. Thompson" provided the most excitement. On June 3, 1882, under command of Captain John McNulty, she left The Dalles at six-thirty in the morning and reached the Upper Cascades in one hundred and twenty-one minutes. This was an average of twenty-three miles an hour, quite respectable time for a stern-wheeler.

Captain McNulty paused only briefly to survey his route, then he pointed the "Thompson's" bow into the boiling rapids. He rang for full power from his engines to gain the greatest possible maneuvering edge. The "Thompson" tore through the twisting six mile channel in twenty seconds less than seven minutes. Her speed for the run was close to a mile a minute and the record she set was never matched.

On the lower river the "Thompson" retained her popularity. After brief service on the Portland-Cascades route, she was placed on the Astoria run. In 1888, she was given a three month refit,

emerging with practically a new hull. Her closest brush with disaster came in 1893 when she sank at Mount Coffin, but she was successfully raised and repaired.

While on the Astoria night run, the "Thompson" left Portland in the evening after dinner, arriving at the down-river city early the next morning. Her passengers, after a restful night aboard arrived refreshed and ready for vacation at the beach or a day of business before embarking for the pleasant return trip.

Her latter days were spent as a spare boat for the Oregon Railway & Navigation Company, successor to the O.S.N. After the turn of the century, the big stern-wheeler found less and less work. Faster boats were built, and anyway, the days of the steamboat were drawing to an inevitable end under competition of railroad and horseless carriage. In 1904, the "R. R. Thompson" went to the dismantler. She was only twenty-six years old, but she'd had a full and satisfactory life.

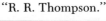

"R. R. Thompson."

THE UNBEATABLE "TELEPHONE"

After their cargo-carrying capacity, stem-wheelers on the Columbia River prided themselves on the luxury and speed with which they could transport passengers . . . but mostly they were proud of their speed. Heyday of the big, gaudy, fast packets came in the mid-1880s and lasted until near the turn of the century. And, although speedsters like the "T. J. Potter" and "Bailey Gatzert" were fast, none ever beat the

"Telephone." She was long and trim when launched in Portland in 1885 by Captain U. B. Scott to run opposition between Portland and Astoria to the "T. J. Potter."

While the "Telephone" earned a reputation for speed, she also seemed bent on destroying herself, first by fire, then by collision. Scarcely two years after launching, she was nearing the Astoria dock at the end of her usual

"Telephone," pride of the Columbia Transportation Co.

I. G. DAVIDSON, PHOTO.   125 FIRST STREET, PORTLAND, OR.

Columbia Transportation Co's Steamer "Telephone."

Length 170 Feet.   Beam 28 Feet.

TIME FROM PORTLAND TO ASTORIA, OREGON, JULY 2ND, 1887—105 MILES—4 HOURS, 34¼ MINUTES.

| Capt. U. B. Scott,
President. | E. A. Seeley,
Agent, Portland. | C. R. Bernard,
Purser. | C. R. Donohoe,
Agent, Astoria. | E. W. Crichton,
Secretary |

Launching of famous "Telephone," 1884.

speed run with one hundred and forty passengers and a crew of thirty-two and Captain Scott at the wheel. Fire suddenly broke out in her oil room and, before the alarm could be passed, was sweeping through the decks. The captain turned her for the beach, signalled the engineer for full throttle and drove the "Telephone" ashore at twenty miles an hour. The passengers leaped over the guards to dry land but Captain Scott, high up in the pilot house and the ladders burned behind him, dove through the window to save himself. The only life lost was a drunk too bemused to find his way out of the cabin.

The Astoria fire department saved the hull and engines and the reborn "Telephone" soon returned, as speedy as ever. In 1892, groping her way up from Astoria on a foggy night, she slammed into a revetment and sank

until only her upper works showed. Raised and patched, she resumed her runs, receiving a new hull in 1903, but losing none of her speed.

The greatest record the "Telephone" set was never bested, even by such fast propellers as the "Georgiana." Downbound from Portland on July 2, 1884, the powerful stern-wheeler made the eighty-five miles in four hours, thirty-four minutes and thirty seconds. The last forty miles was against headwinds and a nasty cross-chop. But Captain Scott hated to be headed by any rival, and so long as he had the "Telephone's" wheel he knew she'd show her heels to any challenger.

In 1909 the Western Pacific Railway, needing a fast ferry between Oakland and San Francisco, bought the "Telephone" and took her down the coast under her own power.

As on the Columbia, no San Francisco Bay rival could touch the "Telephone" for speed. Backing out of the Oakland dock and swinging her slender length around to head for her San Francisco berth, she'd often be minutes behind the Southern Pacific double-ender ferry with a faster getaway. But her wheel would gain speed until the wake streamed out behind like the tail-race of a dam, and the "Telephone" would be discharging passengers before her opponent was fairly tied up at the San Francisco slip.

The junkers got the "Telephone" in 1918. But no competitor ever got her speed trophy and she proudly sported a broom at her masthead for the clean sweeps that masterful piloting and loving care of her engines earned.

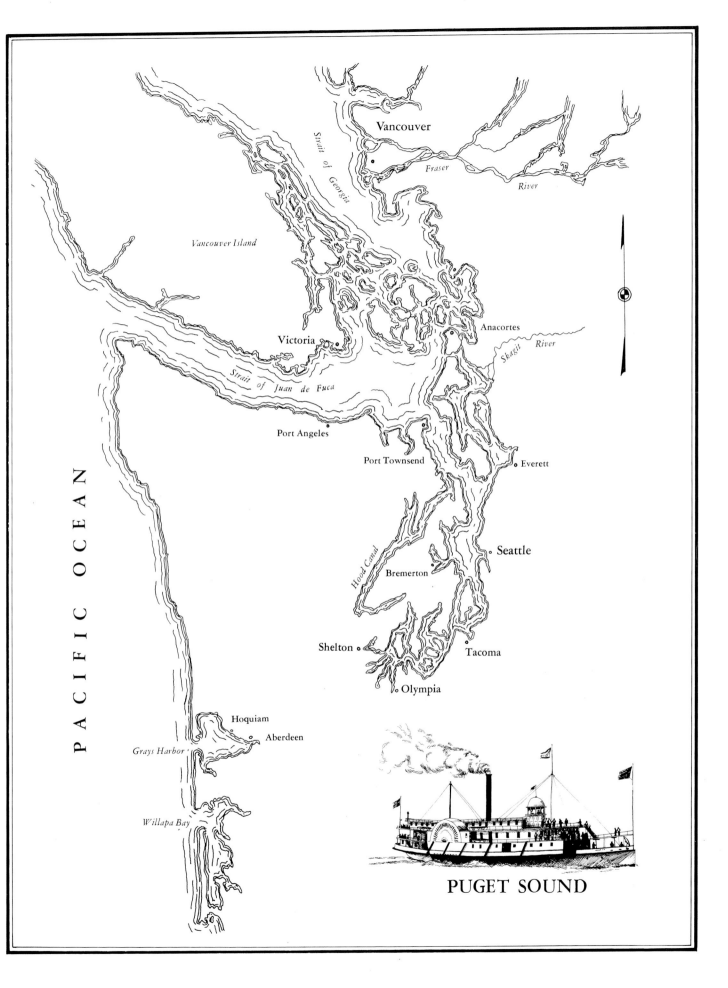

PUGET SOUND

"Multnomah" was fast and economical, serving her owners well on both the Columbia and Puget Sound.

"Multnomah" (1885) was built for Columbia-Willamette River service but was sold to Puget Sound interests when four years old. Until rammed and sunk in 1911, "Multnomah" was a regular boat on the Seattle-Tacoma-Olympia route.

"Modoc" was the last steamer operated on the Columbia by O. R. & N. After the company withdrew from river operations in 1916, "Modoc" was sent to Puget Sound.

Though built on stern-wheel lines, the trim steamer "Wasco" (1887) was a propeller which ran over the Cascades in 1889 to go north to Puget Sound. There she was renamed "Bay City," working as a passenger and excursion boat until she burned in 1903.

Machinery from "Mary Bell" went into "Otter" (1874) when the O.S.N. built her. Transferred to the Sound within a year, she ran as a towboat, passenger-freight combination, and trading boat until 1890, when a collision with "Hassalo" damaged the smaller "Otter" beyond salvage.

"I CHRISTEN THEE . . ."

Hand trucks at the ready, "City of Salem's" roustabouts and a nonchalant passenger pose before turning to. The pyramidal roof on the pilot house was the builder's personal touch.

"Alert," "Economy," "Greyhound," "Success," and "Resolute."

River towns were honored, some of them because local citizens had sunk money into transportation ventures, others because they were principal landings. So plying the Columbia and Willamette were the "Albany," "City of Eugene," "Dalles City," and "Salem."

Occasionally, though, a little whimsy and a lot of realism got mixed up in steamboat naming. Like the inelegant

"Grey Eagle" (left) and "City of Eugene" engaged in log towing on the Willamette around Salem in the late nineties

Plain or fanciful, poetic or prosaic, the names of the steamboat fleet of the Pacific Northwest ring down through the years. They often memorialized civic leaders — Alexander Griggs, W. R. Todd, Frederick K. Billings — or gentle ladies such as Alice, Mable, Gwendoline, and Helen Hale.

Proud owners, hoping to lure business away from their rivals, favored such descriptive names as "Pronto,"

"No Wonder" in Beaver Slough with bowload of cordwood fuel.

"Mud Hen," a stern-wheeler that plodded up and down Beaver Slough, a tributary of the Coquille River, picking her way around and often over sandbars and being scraped by overhanging branches along the narrow route. Or like the "Shoo Fly," "Skedaddle," "Topsy," "Don't Bother Me," and "Rough," all of which performed useful services but whose owners were fairly honest about the lack of queenliness and elegance of their craft.

Reasons for choosing some of the more original names have been forgotten, except in the case of the "No Wonder." She started out sensibly enough in 1877 as the "Wonder," built at Portland by George Washington Weidler as the first log-towing vessel on the Willamette. Waterfront busy-bodies speculated as to how Old Man Weidler got enough money to build her, and why, but the vessel performed so efficiently that when she was rebuilt in 1889 Weidler, tongue in cheek, changed her name to "No Wonder."

She continued to operate for her owners, the Willamette Steam Mills & Lumbering Co., and for Shaver Transportation Company, which purchased her in 1897, retaining her in log-towing and as a training school for pilots and engineers. The "No Wonder" plugged steadily away at her trade until retired and dismantled in 1933, ending a life span of fifty-six years, unusually long for a wooden-hulled steamboat.

In the spring of 1966, the Veteran Steamboatmen's Association paid her honor at their annual Champoeg State Park reunion. Old Man Weidler had been vindicated.

Steamer "No Wonder."

CAPTAIN LEN WHITE, NUMBER ONE RIVERMAN

Written large across the pages of the past are names of men, in their day household words along the rivers, who were heroes to lads then growing up by the Snake and Columbia, much as are astronauts to today's growing dreamers. Men like "Bas" Miller, who brought the "Shoshone" hell-bent down through the Grand Canyon of the Snake. Like Thomas J. Stump, who was captain on every steamboat the Oregon Steam Navigation Company owned. Like John Gates, superb engineer, who invented the hydraulic steering system that saved more than one craft in treacherous rapids. There were other giants: Eph Baughman, W. P. Gray, James W. Troup, Arthur Riggs, John Wolf. But towering over all in courage, ability, and resourcefulness was Captain Leonard White.

Captain White was regarded by his peers as a river pilot born. He could "read" a river. This is no mean feat, and the man who possesses this faculty is regarded with respect bordering on awe. Captain White could tell from the set of the current, from the ripples ahead, from the way the waves curled and broke whether the channel was deep and safe, or whether deadly rock or snag lay hidden below the surface.

By the mid-1850s, pilots had pushed the head of Willamette River navigation as far as Albany, one hundred and eight miles up from Portland. Although Corvallis was only twelve river miles on, it was the other side of the moon so far as cautious rivermen were concerned. Captain White thought differently. He reasoned that if the river flowed past Corvallis, God had put the water there so steamboats could run on it. Captain White forthwith took his boat there, and the grateful burghers of Corvallis had a reception in his honor complete with speeches and presented him the deed to a square block of the city. Corvallis, in return, gained permanent status as a river landing. But Captain White was not finished with the Willamette. In the fall of 1855, despite driftwood and snags that obstructed the narrow, winding channel, he took his "Fenix" to Harrisburg, thirty-three miles above Corvallis. A year later, he was in command of the "James Clinton" when it reached Eugene City, one hundred and seventy-three miles above Portland. For even the dauntless Captain White this was the end of the line. Above, there were more rocks than water.

In 1858 he was hired to command the "Colonel Wright," first steamboat built on the Columbia above The Dalles. The "Wright's" owners intended to cash in on the booming business of hauling miners and supplies to the newly-opened Idaho gold fields, or as close to them as Len White could push a stern-wheeler. He did well. From the mouth of the Snake to Lewiston was one hundred and forty miles, almost all of it roaring white water never before attempted by a steamboat. Captain White changed that by becoming the first to land at Lewiston. A bit later he took the "Colonel Wright" past Lewiston up the Clearwater almost to the forks. Then he essayed the Snake River as far as the mouth of the Grande Ronde, just to see if it could be done.

In 1865, after the Oregon Steam Navigation Company had taken over the fleet of his employers, Captain White lost the argument in a disagreement over salary and quit the new outfit. He turned north, up the Columbia to Little Dalles, sixteen miles short of the Canadian border, near where the forty-ninth parallel crosses. There Cap-

tain White built a steamboat, named it "Forty-Nine," and advertised for passengers for Arrow Lakes and a new gold strike in British Columbia.

Here Captain White's hand played out. The strike fizzled, and though he pushed the "Forty-Nine" more than two hundred miles up the Columbia, fighting ice and lining over rapids, it wasn't a paying proposition. Worn out by overwork, health failing, Captain White sold his boat in 1869 and went to San Francisco, hoping to recover. Within a year he had returned to Portland where he died in the spring of 1870.

Captain White, in less than twenty years, had navigated more uncharted Northwest river waters than any man before him. His only monument is the clear knowledge by every pilot who has followed him of the debt they owe to his pathfinding.

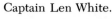

Captain Len White.

WE HOPE THAT YOU ENJOY THIS BOOK . . . and that it will occupy a proud place in your library. We would like to keep you informed about other publications from Schiffer Publishing Ltd.

TITLE OF BOOK: _____

☐ hardcover
☐ paperback

☐ Bought at: _____
☐ Received as gift

COMMENTS: _____

Name (please print clearly) _____

Address _____

City _____ State _____ Zip _____

☐ Please send me a free Schiffer Arts, Antiques & Collectibles catalog.

☐ Please send me a free Schiffer Woodcarving, Woodworking & Crafts catalog

☐ Please send me a free Schiffer Military/Aviation History catalog

☐ Please send me a free Whitford Press Mind, Body & Spirit and Doming Pictorials & Cookbooks catalog.

SCHIFFER BOOKS ARE CURRENTLY AVAILABLE FROM YOUR BOOKSELLER

Printed in the U.S.A.

SCHIFFER PUBLISHING LTD
77 LOWER VALLEY RD
ATGLEN PA 19310-9717

ADVENTURES ON THE SNAKE RIVER

Steamboating in the Pacific Northwest, seldom a tranquil occupation, became downright hazardous on a couple of occasions when two foolhardy attempts were made to bring steamboats down the Snake River through Hells Canyon. By dint of skill and luck both turned out successfully.

First passage was made by the "Shoshone" in 1886. When built at the mouth of Boise River she was planned as a source of much quick revenue in hauling miners and supplies on the middle Snake. But even before she went into service, faster routes to the mines were developed and her owner's dreams went glimmering.

The "Shoshone" was a real steamboat, one hundred and thirty-six feet long and built at great cost, so the deci-

"Norma" was the second of only two steamers to run through Hells Canyon of the Snake. She made the trip in 1895 and served out her days on the Lewiston-Riparia run.

"Norma," built at Bridgeport, Idaho, in 1891.

sion was made to bring her to the Columbia where more profitable runs waited. Captain Sebastian Miller and Chief Engineer Daniel E. Buchanan drew the assignment and were sent from Portland to Huntington, Oregon, near where the "Shoshone" had lain idle for a couple of years. When they arrived they found her pine lumber seams had opened. With no caulking materials at hand, Captain Miller rigged pumps and flooded the decks until the gaps swelled shut.

A cargo of cordwood fuel was stacked aboard, the engines were checked, candles were set alight in the hold to detect leaks, and Captain Miller rang for power. Copper Ledge Falls boiled a couple of hundred yards downstream. Before the boat was properly under control, Captain Miller found himself in the grip of the river. Three times the "Shoshone" spun around before she straightened out and pointed her bow toward the verge. She tipped, shuddered, and plunged down wiping out eight feet of bow and portions of the paddle wheel.

Captain Miller landed. A couple of days were spent repairing the damage and the unruly Snake was faced again. A number of misadventures and seven days later the "Shoshone" drifted quietly to a landing at Lewiston, some two hundred miles from the beginning.

Twenty-five years later Captain William P. Gray took the "Norma" through the same ordeal but he profited from Captain Miller's experience and waited for high water. At the end of his week-long trip Captain Gray wrote, "I know from personal experience that it is not practical to navigate the Box Canyon section of the Snake River and never will be." At least so far as stern-wheelers are concerned, he was absolutely correct.

THE WHITE ELEPHANT THAT FLOATED

Grandest vessel on Okanagan Lake "Sicamous," for almost a quarter century the premium passenger and freight carrier between Penticton, B. C. and upper lake points.

Some mighty classy steamboats ran on the waters of Puget Sound and the Columbia River—high style passenger packets like the "Telephone," "Daisy Ainsworth," "Wide West," and "North Pacific." Few were as magnificent as the "Olympian" and few were as financially impractical. She, with her sister ship "Alaskan," was conceived by Henry Villard. This financial genius, who once monopolized the Northwest's rail and water transportation system, must have suffered a lapse of common-sense when he ordered the pair constructed in Delaware.

Both were iron-hulled side-wheelers of magnificent proportions. The "Olympian" was two hundred and sixty-two feet long and forty feet wide. The "Alaskan" was fourteen feet longer. The "Olympian" arrived first on Puget Sound in 1884. Villard put her on the Victoria-Tacoma route under his Oregon Railway & Navigation Com-

pany house flag. She was something to write home about. Incandescent lamps, a rarity at that time, reflected off polished mahogany tables in the great dining saloon. Brass beds and glistening mirrors, carpets and running water graced each of the fifty staterooms. She was, to say the least, luxurious. And she was so expensive to operate that she never made a profit, either on the Sound or on the Columbia, where Villard later put her.

About the greatest service the "Olympian" performed occurred in January 1886. On the twenty-second of that month a blizzard struck the gorge west of Hood River. Snow drifted across the O.R.& N. rail tracks halting

"Olympian" breaking ice.

all traffic. The Columbia River was frozen tight, impassable to wooden-hulled river steamers. The west-bound Pacific Express had reached Hood River that morning with passengers, freight and mail. She was ordered to remain there while means were sought to rescue her beleagured passengers and those expected on following trains.

The "Olympian" provided the solution. She drew nine feet of water and her iron hull would be strong enough to battle the ice blockade.

Let F. B. Gill, railroad historian, writing in 1914 of the rescue, tell the story. . . .

"She made two attempts to reach the trains, the first time having to turn back. Leaving Portland on the second attempt at seven thirty A.M., on the twenty-sixth the "Olympian" first encountered trouble at the Vancouver bar where the river was frozen solid to the bottom, but the steamer chiseled her way through, running into ice as far as she could go, then backing out and trying again."

Slowly the steamer made progress, the swell from her paddle wheels breaking the floes so the current could carry the ice downstream. A short distance above Vancouver the "Olympian" nearly met disaster. She had battled about halfway through a ten mile long ice gorge.

"The whole gorge started and the engines unfortunately were caught on the center, leaving her practically helpless," Gill writes. "For nearly an hour and a half she was carried down the river, when she was thrown into an eddy under the sand bar a short distance above Vancouver where the steamer lodged against solid ice. Both anchors were put out, but dragged, and it was the eddy which held her."

The gorge passed downstream during the night and by nine the next morning the captain considered it safe to try again. The "Olympian" bucked through ice jams at Fisher's Landing, Rooster Rock and Cape Horn. By evening, she was at Dodson's fish wheel, four miles below Bonneville. The captain would go no further; a short distance upstream ice was piled twenty feet above the river surface.

On the morning of January twenty-eighth trains at Hood River and The Dalles were ordered to try to reach Dodson's. The railroad's superintendent, with sixty-five laborers brought along on the "Olympian," slashed a path through the brush from the rail track to the bank where the sidewheeler lay. By ten that morning one hundred and seventy-five grateful passengers, along with mail and freight, had been transferred to the "Olympian." At three-forty P.M., she was back at Ash Street dock in Portland, having lost only a little paint during the ordeal.

The next day she returned upriver with passengers and mail for the East. On the thirtieth, the tracks were cleared through the gorge and normal rail schedules resumed.

Villard, anxious to be rid of his white elephant, chartered her out briefly to a company in the Alaska trade. She shortly was back on his hands and in 1890 she was sent to the Portland boneyard. Other owners in 1906 resurrected the bedraggled old queen, hoping to return her to service on the East Coast. She ran aground in the Straits of Magellan, the land of perpetual snow and ice.

STR. "SPOKANE," ALIAS U.S. GUNBOAT

Steamboats often were called on for unusual duties outside the routine of passenger and freight hauling and one of the strangest assignments fell to the "Spokane." She served the U.S. Army as a gunboat to help put down an Indian uprising during the Bannock War of 1878.

The "Spokane," only eight months off the stocks at Celilo, where she had been built in the record time of thirty-two days, six hours for the Oregon

"Spokane" was built for the Oregon Steam Navigation Co. in 1878, and acquired by the Oregon Railway & Navigation Co. in 1879.

Sacked wheat, wagon hauled to the bank of the Snake, goes aboard the "Spokane" for transshipment to the railhead at Riparia.

Steam Navigation Company, was on the Snake River run between Lewiston and Riparia when the southern Idaho Bannock Indians jumped the reservation. Gathering allies, the braves moved toward the Columbia River through northeastern Oregon, hoping to cross into Washington Territory and join up with three thousand, five hundred restless Yakimas, also ripe for an uprising.

The Army's 2nd Infantry, stationed at Fort Walla Walla, had to stop the merger. General Frank Wheaton commandeered the "Spokane," placed nineteen regulars and forty-two volunteers aboard, and armed them with a Gatling gun, a small howitzer and rifles. Sacks of flour on deck provided breastworks.

The "Spokane" was assigned to patrol the Columbia between Umatilla

"Spokane" at the Riparia railroad bridge on the lower Snake River. "Spokane" mostly ran between Lewiston and railroad points as a transfer boat. She burned at the Lewiston dock in 1922.

and Arlington. Thirteen miles below Umatilla, the Bannocks had swum three hundred horses to the Washington side and were attempting to get another two hundred over. The "Spokane" rounded to and fired, frightening off the Indians on the north bank. Troops landed to pursue them and to gather up abandoned livestock.

A few miles downstream, at Thanksgiving Island near Arlington, the "Spokane" surprised another band of Indians attempting a crossing. The volunteers and soldiers bombarded both sides of the river, driving off the braves. A fleet of canoes on the south bank was destroyed and more horses were rounded up. Some were brought aboard the stern-wheeler.

Her mission accomplished, the "Spokane" returned to Umatilla, sul-lenly watched from the river bank by the chastened Indians. The Bannock War trickled off into minor encounters and before long the U.S. Infantry pushed the warriors back to their reservations.

The "Spokane" resumed her prosaic daily run hauling passengers and freight between Lewiston and the railhead at Riparia, seventy-five miles down the Snake. She had no other notable adventures but none were needed. Her few days of fame and glory sustained her and often, as she drowsed at a landing under the hot Snake Canyon sun, she must have been remembering the whistle of bullets, the shouts of command and the angry challenges of paint-daubed warriors in the last of Oregon's Indian wars.

"Spokane" and the Corps of Engineers' snag boat "Asotin" share space at a north bank landing in the neighborhood of Almota.

FINISHED WITH ENGINES

Twin stacks were rare on Pacific Northwest steamers. The powerful tug "Jean" had four engines and a dual stern-wheel, each half capable of independent operation.

First, in 1886, there was "N. S. Bentley." Then, ten years later, "Albany" emerged from the original product. The final reincarnation in 1906 was "Georgie Burton," which hung onto her identity for another forty years.

"Georgie Burton" at Vancouver, 1936.

Nearly one hundred years passed from a spring day in 1850, when the "Columbia," first paddlewheeler in Oregon waters, received her baptism at Astoria, until another day in the spring of 1947 saw the launching of the "Portland" and with it the end to an era. In that span of time, more than half a thousand steamboats traveled the rivers of the Columbia system and the coastal streams and inland lakes of Oregon. Plodding, work-a-day towboats, sleek, nobby palace packets, jerry-built mechanized flatboats: they were part and parcel of a time that will not come again.

None has come forward to save the memory. The "Jean," last but one of the hundreds, idles at the Western Transportation Company moorage under Portland's Steel Bridge, stripped of machinery, demeaned to a carpenter shop. The "Portland" is at work for a while yet, shouldering her stately way through the harbor's scurrying diesels like a grande dame among a covey of schoolgirls. When her days are ended her owners, the Port of Portland Commission, have said she will become a museum piece and so be preserved.

Such was the plan for the "Georgie Burton." A few who foresaw the passing of the stern-wheelers determined she should be a reminder of the age. A moorage was to be secured at The Dalles, a fitting place, and on March 20, 1947, the "Georgie Burton" made her final voyage. Her decks were crowded with passengers — old time captains and pilots, pursers, engineers, mud clerks, men whose lives had been wedded to the river — when she let go her lines and whistled goodbye to Portland.

People lined the Columbia's banks to mark the passage. Above The Dalles, the "Georgie Burton" nudged into temporary berth at the foot of Celilo Canal to wait until a proper place was pre-

Wreck of "Georgie Burton," 1948.

pared and she would become a land-locked museum. There, below Celilo, the great May flood of 1948 caught the "Georgie Burton" and in a few wild moments all the fine plans ended. The surge of the Columbia's rising water, carrying power that had been building since the headwaters a thousand miles above, snapped the "Burton's" moorings. Helplessly, she whirled into mid-stream, crushing herself against a concrete embankment to lie with her back broken, beyond saving.

She had been a good boat for forty years, steady, reliable, a familiar profile on the Willamette and Columbia. Perhaps her finish was fitting, that she should end not torn from her element and stranded on shore, but giving herself back to the river she had served.

THE ONLY ONE OF HER KIND

Steamboatmen were the world's greatest string savers or its greatest sentimentalists. Anything that could be converted, salvaged, or adapted from an older craft was put to use on a successor. New deckhouses were built on old hulls; ancient boilers powered new engines; whistles, bells, wheels, and miscellaneous hardware rotated among the river boats for decades.

So it was with the "Logger." Her story begins in 1903 when Captain U. B. Scott built the stern-wheel packet "Telegraph" at Everett, Washington, for service between that city and Seattle. She served well until 1912 when she fell victim to one of the more memorable Puget Sound marine disasters. The "Telegraph" was idle at Colman Dock when the Alaska Steamship Co. iron liner "Alameda," mishandled through an incredible mixup of signals between bridge and engine room, smashed through the pier to cut the wooden-hulled "Telegraph" almost in two and sink her where she lay.

The wreck was raised and repaired, her single cylinder engines were compounded, and she was sold to new owners. Renamed the "Olympian," the steamer was placed on the daily Seattle-Olympia-Tacoma run. She was not a success in this service and finally was sent to the Columbia River.

There, on the Portland-The Dalles route, the "Olympian" soon found herself an anachronism. Trucks on the newly opened Columbia River highway cut sharply into river freight so the "Olympian's" owners established the forerunner of today's roll-on roll-off hauling. Loaded motor trucks, placed on the deck in Portland, drove off at the upriver terminal direct to the consignee's business house. The scheme did not prove profitable. The "Olympian" then ran brief competition against the speedy "Georgiana" on the Portland-Astoria passenger-freight run but in 1921 was removed from service and laid up.

In 1924, Smith Transportation Co., Rainier, Oregon, acquired her, stripped off the house and machinery and installed them in a new one hundred and fifty-six foot wooden hull. This rebirth, built solely to tow log rafts, was christened the "Logger." In one respect, the "Logger" was unique. She was the only stern-wheeler ever built on the river to run on hog fuel.

Hog fuel is chipped sawmill waste. It is dusty, splintery, and in all ways ornery to handle. But it is economical. After 1930, Shaver Transportation Co., which had acquired the "Logger" with several other boats through merger with the Smith Company, found operating her was a constant problem and challenge. When she finally opened and sank at her moorings in 1938, no attempt was made at salvage. She was stripped of metal and the hull now lies under many feet of fill that makes up the Waterway Terminals Company property on Portland's waterfront.

What's left of the "Logger," ex-"Olympian," ex-"Telegraph?" Only her name board, enshrined with many others in the marine museum at Champoeg.

Steamer "Logger."

"Claire," below the Hawthorne Bridge, downbound from West Linn with a paper barge.

The inscription on this monument on the banks of the Willamette at Lake Oswego reads:

Fog Bell
Steamer "Claire"
1918-1952
Presented by
Western Transportation Co.

"Claire" clears the old Morrison Bridge.

The "paper mill fleet," "Claire" on the left. Owned by Western Transportation Co., a Crown Zellerbach Corporation subsidiary, the fleet handled towing chores between company mills and steamer docks and warehouses in Portland.

"Claire" at Champoeg Landing for the Veteran Steamboatmens' Reunion, 1952.

THE MOST-TRAVELED STEAMBOAT

In the four decades she served on waters of the West, the "Wilson G. Hunt" probably traveled farther at the whim of numerous owners yet consistently turned more profits than most of her contemporaries. The "Hunt's" days began and ended in San Francisco Bay but the forty intervening years also saw her on Puget Sound, the Columbia River, and British Columbia's Lower Fraser River.

The "Hunt" was a stout boat. She proved that by surviving a winter passage around Cape Horn that almost

"Wilson G. Hunt."

foundered her. Agents of the California Steam Navigation Company had bought her shortly after launching in New York where she had been built for the Coney Island trade. The 1849 California gold rush had created heavy demands for anything that would float to transport miners and supplies from San Francisco to the mining regions. Though the C.S.N. paid dearly for the "Hunt," and the cost of bringing her around from the East Coast was high, the profit potential was worth it. The "Hunt" did not disappoint. Placed at once on the Sacramento River route, she cleared one million dollars in a single season, and continued to run profitably for the next nine years.

In 1858, the "Hunt" began her peregrinations. She journeyed north to Victoria, B.C., and from August until October carried miners headed for Fraser River diggings and the mails to New Westminster. The next several years saw the "Hunt" successfully plying the Olympia-Victoria run.

Gold brought her to the Sacramento, gold kept her on the Fraser, and it was the clamor of miners for transportation to the Idaho gold strikes that took the "Hunt" to the Columbia in 1862.

The obliging side-wheeler turned a handsome profit for her new owners, the Oregon Steam Navigation Company, on the Cascades route. Her capacious cabins easily accommodated up to three hundred passengers and her freight deck could handle a hundred head of cattle and general cargo as well. In 1869, the O.S.N., its Columbia River monopoly assured, turned covetous attention to Puget Sound. There the company sent the "Hunt" to run competition to Messrs. Finch & Wright who, with the "Eliza Anderson," had a firm hold on the profitable Olympia-Seattle-Port Townsend-Victoria run.

The price war raged until Finch & Wright, seeing profits erode, bought the "Hunt" from a willing O.S.N. and sold her off to San Francisco interests.

Back down the coast went the "Hunt," to dutifully work another seven years. Then Captain John Irving, who was having competition troubles of his own on the Fraser River, remembered the "Wilson G. Hunt." He located her in the Bay and thus, twenty years after she first had docked at New Westminster the dogged old side-wheeler was back in Canadian waters. Irving ran her for a while against the Hudson's Bay Company steamer "Enterprise," sold her, bought her back and remained her owner almost to the end of her days.

But the "Wilson G. Hunt" had one more ocean voyage to make. Forty years old, too expensive to operate and maintain, she was sold to Cohn & Company, ship breakers, who did business, of all places, in San Francisco. Under her own power, her anachronistic steeple engine functioning as faithfully as the day she was launched, the "Hunt" pointed her bow for a final time in the direction of the Golden Gate. She was destroyed in 1890 for her iron; the memories they could not destroy.

"GEORGIANA," TRANSITION BOAT

"Georgiana," as fine a boat as many of the stern-wheelers, formed the transition between steam and diesel on the Columbia. She was built for speed rather than comfort. Freight for lower river hamlets with no access to civilization except by water was almost as important as the passengers she carried.

As the heyday of the steamboat waned and these proud queens of the river gave way to the inevitabilities of cheaper rail and truck freight hauling, they did not leave the scene with a wheeze and a whimper. Though they saw freight taken over by the new transportation systems and passengers lured away by faster, if far less comfortable, passenger trains and automobiles, the stern-wheelers took their own time about retiring.

And in the leaving, they proved they yet could show their heels to the fastest of the new propeller boats. For no matter how hard their captains pushed them, latter-day passenger packets such as the "America" and the "Georgiana" never bested the Portland-Astoria records set by such paddle wheel racers as the "Telephone" and "Telegraph."

Best-remembered of the lower-river propeller passenger boats was the "Georgiana." Three ladies of that name were equally honored at the 1914 launching ceremonies: Mrs. H. L. Pittock, wife of *The Oregonian's* publisher, and her granddaughters, Georgiana Leadbetter and Georgiana Gantenbein. This was the second such accolade for Mrs. Pittock. The "Georgie Burton," a fine and long-lived stern-wheeler, had borne her maiden name at its 1906 christening.

The "Georgiana" was designed purposely for Harkins Transportation Company's passenger trade; she carried a minimum of freight. Her one dollar fare between Portland and Astoria was meant to attract those who could not afford the higher-priced rail ride.

Though small (only one hundred and forty-five feet long with a twenty-two and one-half foot beam), the "Georgiana" was nicely appointed. The Oregonian compared her to a yacht. Main lounge and smoking rooms were bright and pleasant. Pullman-type seats beside large windows let passengers enjoy the scenery in comfort. Galley and dining rooms were purposely small. As a day boat, the "Georgiana" served few meals; passengers were encouraged to carry a lunch.

Up and down the Columbia the "Georgiana" shuttled, making Washington landings on the downriver morning run and Oregon stops on the afternoon return. Her rival was the "Astorian" (ex-"Nisqually" of Puget Sound) and on an April day in 1920 the two boats faced off. Smoke pluming from their stacks, they chased each other the entire one hundred and ten miles from Portland to Astoria. "Georgiana" made five scheduled landings, "Astorian" two, yet the former won the race — five hours and forty-five minutes berth to berth, besting her competitor by three minutes.

That afternoon "Astorian" evened the score, though "Georgiana's" supporters cried "Foul"! Their boat had made nine scheduled landings to "Astorian's" two and had added a stop at Linnton to fuel up.

It was 1939 before the "Georgiana" left the lower river, profits eroded by land transportation. In a quarter of a century spent at her trade she had outlasted competition boats and had been the instrument of transition between paddle wheel and propeller.

There was another season left to her, though. Brightened by a coat of glistening white paint and under new ownership she was renamed "Lake Bonneville" and put on the Portland-Bonneville Dam excursion run. It was a lost cause. There was not enough trade to continue the venture for long and the handsome old craft was sent to retirement. Finally she was beached near Post Office Bar on Sauvie Island, within sight of the channel she had plied countless times, until the hull slowly sanded over and settled into a fitting, final resting place.

"HENDERSON," LAST OF A BREED

It's a sad thing to see a lady come upon hard times. The old dash and charm may not be fully gone; a regal aura may still shine through her fustiness. But still it is hard to accept.

So with the stern-wheeler "Henderson," last of a great fleet of wooden-hulled river steamers, her bones now on the river bank at Columbia City, Oregon.

"Henderson" with "Hassalo's" whistle.

When the Standard Oil tanker "F. S. Follis" missed the Willamette River entrance channel, the Shaver fleet muscled her free. Full power is applied by the propeller tugs "Chinook" and "James W.," and the stern-wheelers "Portland" and "Henderson." The little "Echo" stands by.

There was talk of saving her for a marine museum but those plans fell through. So did the scheme to remove her machinery, make the engine room over into a machine shop and her cabin deck into living quarters. But there is money to be made from scrap metal and it costs something in labor and materials to rework a boat's spaces.

So finally she was burned and only

"Henderson" (1912) and "Portland" (1947) staged the last Columbia River steamboat race in 1952. The wooden-hulled "Henderson" won.

the hull remains. That, and a few mementos like her big steering wheel and the name boards saved for display some day by the Oregon Historical Society, and the pitman rods and the metal paddle wheel fittings removed by an old friend to be stored against the day when these things will be a curiosity.

The "Henderson" lived unusually long for a wooden ship. From her launching in 1901 as the "M. F. Henderson," through sinking and rebuilding in 1912 (she lost her initials then),

Stalwarts of the steamboat fleet, such as "Henderson," were in demand to move powerless ships through Portland's harbor bridges during World War II.

Though forty years old in 1952, "Henderson" yet had enough glamor to star in the movie *Bend of the River* under the stage name "River Queen." Given a fresh coat of paint and a couple of prop prairie schooners, she became a leading lady.

Lawrence Barber Photograph

"Henderson" leads in the last steamboat race on the Columbia.

another sinking in 1950, and victory in a brief but memorable race against the "Portland" for a filming of the movie "Bend of the River," she towed log rafts, pushed ships and barges and performed well all the chores expected of her. Mostly, all she needed was an occasional haul out for bottom repair and caulking.

The end came for the "Henderson" near Astoria late in 1956. The gracious old lady, a grain ship alongside, was smashed by surging seas against the unyielding steel sides of her tow. Her house and upper works were wrenched out of line and she suffered such general damage that insurance underwriters and the Coast Guard denied her permission to return to service.

"A constructive total loss" said Captain Homer T. Shaver, General Manager of Shaver Transportation Company, her builders and operators.

The insurance money was taken, the "Henderson" was sold, and an era ended.

ENTER "SHAVER," EXIT "WESTERN"

Almost no Pacific Northwest stern-wheeler escaped major rebuilding or considerable overhaul during its lifetime. Fires, boiler explosions, collisions, groundings, and normal wear and tear conspired to require occasional alterations. Like as not the vessel was lengthened or re-engined at the same time to allow for bigger freight loads, more speed, greater pushing power, or a combination of all three. The stern-wheeler "Shaver" was no different from the others, but when her transformation occurred she established a trend that altered towboat design on every river in the United States.

The "Shaver" left the ways of Port-

Launching of steamer "Shaver," 1908.

Astoria abeam, "M. F. Henderson" and "Shaver" bring a "cigar raft" down to a waiting ocean tug for the haul to southern California.

land Shipbuilding Company in 1908 flying the house flag of Shaver Transportation Company, the "Red Collar Line." Of standard Columbia River design, she was the seventh stern-wheeler in the company fleet. Into her spanking new hull went a set of engines that already had seen nearly half a century of service. Taken from the twin-stacked "J. M. Hannaford," bought by the Shavers from the SP&S Railroad which had built the vessel as a workboat during railroad construction days, these engines had first powered a paddle wheeler on the Red River of the South back in 1859.

During the Civil War this craft, named the "Arkansas Chief," served as a Federal gunboat on the Mississippi.

Some years later, the "Chief" was laid up at St. Louis and it was there the railroad bought the hulk to get engines for the "Hannaford." So, when the Shaver acquired it, the old poppet valve power plant already had been at work for fifty-one years.

It is difficult to improve on the efficient design of a Columbia River stern-wheeler. A powerful, wide paddle wheel bites deeply into the water, providing leverage and thrust against the river's power. The long, narrow hull, deep forward and shallow aft, gives the pilot a fine maneuvering touch to handle ships and barges in current and wind. Plenty of rudder surface, provided by monkey rudders forward of the stern-wheel and by standard rudders behind, gives complete and immediate response whether the boat is going ahead or backing.

But the Shavers changed this concept in 1926. In so doing they created a new dimension in towboat power. To J. H. Johnstone, Seattle naval architect, fell the problem of design. The "Shaver" was hauled out of the water and her stern-wheel was removed. So were the ancient steam engines which by now had been in service for sixty-seven years. In their place went two four hundred horsepower diesels. The fan-tail was remodeled, the cylinder supports were removed. Under the stern were built two tunnels to carry propeller shafts. The "Shaver" emerged with essential hull structure unchanged, but she had become the first twin-screw, tunnel-stern diesel towboat in the United States.

The changeover cost about one hundred thousand dollars, and wiseacres on the waterfront scoffed at the creation. But the new boat went about her assignments efficiently and steadily, only suffering fire damage to the upperworks in 1943 that required

major rebuilding. Before the vessel was sold, some twenty years after, she had repaid the one hundred thousand dollar investment with interest.

Soon after her conversion, the Marietta (Ohio) Iron Works and the Atlas Imperial Engine Company obtained the "Shaver's" plans and a towboat of this type was built on the Mississippi River, forerunner of the fleets of the future.

Shortly after World War II, the "Shaver" was sold to Western Transportation Company, which renamed her the "Western." Finally, in 1956, after forty-eight years of labor, the venerable craft was retired and sold to owners who planned to convert her into a floating restaurant. The scheme fell through, and she lay largely untended in Oregon Slough until the spring freshet of 1960 sank her. The old lady finally was burned, by accident or design. All that remains is a charred transom washing in a slough's backwater as a reminder of the Columbia River steamboat that influenced river transportation for all time.

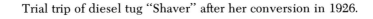
Trial trip of diesel tug "Shaver" after her conversion in 1926.

"Shaver" towing U.S.S. "Constitution" in 1934.

Ladies' cabin in "Wide West."   Forward cabin of "Wide West."

Ladies' cabin in "Joseph Kellogg."

Men's cabin on "City of Salem."

Dining Saloon of "T. J. Potter."

"T. J. Potter."

A harbor full of welcomers and "T. J. Potter" salute the battleship "Oregon" on her return home after her Spanish-American War heroics.

"T. J. POTTER," QUEEN OF THE EXCURSION BOATS

The ocean shore resorts that grew up along the northern Oregon beaches near Seaside and Gearhart in the late 1860s and onward, and later on the Long Beach peninsula just north of the mouth of the Columbia River, became the watering places for Portland's fashionable people whose handsome homes were occupied during the summer season by wives and families. Shortly, the popularity of the resorts drew crowds of weekend picnickers until a whole new fleet of fast steamboats was needed to accommodate the traffic.

The most smartly appointed, and the boat that soon became the accepted way to travel, was the "T. J. Potter." She carried forward the tradition of elegance established on the middle river by the "Wide West" whose upper works, with some modification, were placed upon the finely moulded hull that was launched at Portland in 1888 as the "Potter." The changes were necessary because the "Wide West" was a stern-wheeler and the "Potter" was designed as a side-wheel steamer, with delicately fret-worked paddle boxes that looked like a pattern in old lace.

A grand staircase, the landing boasting the largest plate-glass mirror in the Northwest, swept upward to the saloon from the lower deck. A grand piano

encased in bird's-eye maple, a paneled dining room, tables set with linen and silver, and a cuisine that rivaled any of Portland's finer restaurants made travel a pleasure. The trip always seemed far too short.

The "T. J. Potter" was on the Portland-Astoria run for the first season after her launching. Then her owners, the Oregon Railway and Navigation Company, sent her to Puget Sound to run competition with the Seattle Steam Navigation and Transportation Company's fast "Bailey Gatzert." This

Pictures of her crew surround the center photo of "T. J. Potter."

"T. J. Potter" meets the narrow-guage "Clamshell Railroad" at Megler, Washington.

proved quite an experience for the "Potter's" passengers. She was a river boat born and bred and, at the first sign of a swell, she rolled ponderously from side to side, lifting first one paddle and then the other out of the water.

Sent back to the Columbia, the "Potter" made her stately way between Astoria and Portland for another twenty-five years, undergoing a rebuilding in 1901 which increased her length from two hundred and thirty to two hundred and thirty-four feet and her tonnage from six hundred and fifty-

nine to one thousand and seventeen. In 1916, the fine old boat was condemned for passenger use. For a few more years she occasionally was used as a barracks boat for construction crews. Then, in 1921 (some say 1925), she was towed to Young's Bay near Astoria and burned for her metal. Even now, at low tide, her bleached bones are visible on the mudflats, a sad reminder of the halcyon days when a trip on the "T. J. Potter" was an occasion to remember.

IF IT'S WET ENOUGH, IT'S DEEP ENOUGH

There always was some doubt in people's minds that the "Chester" really needed water to navigate in. A heavy dew, or even a fairly damp trail, would have been sufficent, they said. But that was the way the Kellogg boys had it figured. They wanted a boat with the shallowest possible draft to service settlers along the Cowlitz River, an unpredictable stream at best, so far as depth was concerned. The amount of water fluctuated from rainstorm to rainstorm, and sand and gravel bars compounded a pilot's woes.

First boat on the Cowlitz was the "Toledo," which served the run from Kelso up the Cowlitz for better than twenty years before she was wrecked, but she drew too much water to give year long service. So, when the Kellogs were compelled to replace her in 1897, they asked Joseph Supple to correct the matter. He succeeded so well that the "Chester" locally became the shallowest draft boat devised. She drew a scant foot of water and seldom bothered about the formalities of landing at a dock. Farmers simply drove their wagons into the stream, the "Chester" pulled alongside, and passengers and freight were transferred with a minimum of trouble.

According to some, the "Chester's" hull design was so practical it was copied for shallow draft steamers on the

Yukon and other Alaskan gold rush streams.

Captain Joseph Kellogg was a man who knew his steamboats, and he knew a few other things, too. Shortly after arriving in Oregon in 1848, he joined forces with Lot Whitcomb and William Torrence to lay out the town of Milwaukie and build a sawmill. To get rid of the lumber Kellogg built a schooner, loaded it for California, and traded vessel and cargo for a brig. Shortly this craft had earned enough to pay for a bark, and the sawmill business boomed to the point where two ships were shuttling back and forth between the Columbia River and San Francisco Bay.

Soon this venture lost its challenge and Captain Kellogg sold out to enter a partnership and build the largest flour mill of its time in the state. Before long his interests were expanding again. He first built a steamboat, then the turning basin at Oregon City, opened navigation on the Tualatin River, built the canal that connected the river with Sucker (now Oswego) Lake, and bought and platted the townsite of Oswego.

In 1870, at the age of fifty-eight, Captain Kellogg and others formed the Willamette River Transportation Company. He superintended the building of two stern-wheelers for the firm, then sold his interests to tackle the Cowlitz under the name of the Joseph Kellogg Transportation Company.

His brothers, Ed and Orrin, joined the venture. Under the company title the sturdy "Chester" served the trade until World War I compelled her layup, and the Cowlitz saw the last of the paddle wheelers.

"Chester" loading in a few inches of water.

PRIDE OF PUGET SOUND

Every so often a visitor to Puget Sound will be jolted out of his serene contemplation of the effulgence of that water wonderland to clutch at the arm of his native host, point, and gasp in astonishment, "What's *that*?" At which his companion will gaze with pity at the untutored outlander and reply, a shade condescendingly, "*That* is a stern-wheeler."

And sure enough it is. The question is a natural one, for stern-wheelers

The U.S. Army Corps of Engineers' snagboat "W. T. Preston" in 1970.

today are a rarity. Few exist. A couple are cruise boats on the Mississippi, another is a working towboat on the Columbia, and then there's the "W. T. Preston."

The "Preston" is one of an extensive fleet operated by the Corps of Engineers, but she is the only one to sport a paddlewheel. And her job is as unusual as her appearance. The "Preston" is a snagboat, filling a role that is strictly utilitarian but one that is of more than passing importance to the water-oriented people of Puget Sound.

Snags and deadheads are the bane of existence to commercial fishermen, pleasure boaters, ferry men, and cargo boatmen who proliferate on the Sound and its tributary waters. Partially or wholly submerged, waiting to rip through hulls or destroy propellers, these lethal navigation hazards must be removed before lives and vessels become their victims. This is the work of the "Preston."

From Blaine at the Canadian line to Shelton at the southern end of Puget Sound, the "Preston" ranges, occasionally poking her prow into the Swinomish, Stillaquamish, Skagit, Duwamish, Puyallup, and other channels in search of danger-laden flotsam.

A prime responsibility of the Corps is maintenance of navigable waterways. Since 1885, in discharging its duty, the Corps has operated three snagboats on Puget Sound. First, was the "Skagit," which functioned until replaced in 1914 by the "Swinomish."

When this craft was retired fifteen years later her steam-powered engines were transferred to the newly built "W. T. Preston."

From paddle wheel to the front of her deckhouse the "Preston" appears to be a typical stern-wheel steamer, but there the similarity ends. The forward deck is given over to a maze of machinery. Towering over all is a seventy foot derrick with hoisting engine capable of handling sixty tons of weight. A one and a quarter cubic yard clam-shell bucket for maintenance dredging can be attached to the derrick boom. Two sturdy steel "spuds," extending through the hull into the channel bottom, securely position the boat while she works.

Though the "Preston" never was designed for speed, she did show her heels on a few occasions to rival paddlers in staged contests. Her best racing pace was twelve knots, but her working range is more like seven. This reduces to about a five knot crawl when the sea kicks up for her wide, flat hull topped by a bulky superstructure makes her an unhandy boat in heavy weather.

With all her blunt lines and work-a-day appearance, the "Preston" occupies a unique place in the affections of Puget Sounders. They enjoy watching the waterfall of her seventeen foot wheel; the chime of her whistle and the whoosh, whoosh of her exhausts are music. For they know full well that when the "W. T. Preston" is gone at last from the scene no more like her will pass that way again.

Five-Finger Rapids, one of the more formidable obstacles on the Yukon, is approached on an upstream run by the "Ora." She, with her sisters "Flora" and "Nora," was built to carry prospectors bound for the diggings across Lake Bennett.

The Stikine River was a challenge to white water men, but steamboats regularly served settlements along its banks. At Wrangell, at the Stikine's mouth, steamboats met freighters from the States. This was also a convenient stop on the Inside Passage for steamers headed for the Yukon. At least fifteen paddle wheelers are visible in this 1898 scene.

"Columbian" of the Canadian Development Co. and the Yukon Flyer Lines' "El Dorado" leave Dawson on July 4, 1899, in a race for Whitehorse Rapids.

At the height of the Alaskan gold stampede and for a few years following, the Canadian Development Co. and successor firms operated a fleet of steamers on the Yukon. These four, hauled out for the winter in 1902 at Whitehorse, Yukon Territory, were built at Victoria and steamed north under their own power in 1898.

Numerous steamers from Puget Sound and the Columbia weathered the long ocean tow to the Yukon River to serve the hordes of gold seekers of '98. This aggregation, led by Portland Captain George M. Shaver (fifth from left, back row), is en route down the Yukon from Lake Laberge, winter layup before the Dawson City boatyard was built.

By the time Yukon-bound goldseekers had struggled over Chilkoot Pass from Skagway as far as Bennett, British Columbia, they were ready to board waiting boats with cries of gladness. Rather than pay the cross-lake fare, some built sailing scows of whip-sawed planks for the long float to Carcross and beyond.

"Nora" and other steamers operated on Lake Bennett, Taku Arm, Atlin Lake and the Yukon River interchangably for several seasons during the height of the rush.

Built in Seattle in 1885, the eighty-five foot "Alaskan" spent most of her career on Canada's Stikine River.

LIFE AND TIMES OF THE "NEW WORLD"

Steamer "New World."

Resourcefulness was a necessary item in the character of steamboat skippers who wanted to hold their commands in the cut and run days of steamboating, and few showed more of it than Captain Ned Wakeman. His command was the "New World," built at New York in 1850 for the Hudson River passenger trade. Debts plagued the owner before she was fairly in service, the courts seized her, and sheriff's deputies were placed aboard to enforce the edict.

Captain Wakeman furtively loaded

stores and fuel, got the deputies drunk, slipped the lines and hightailed it for the open sea, pausing only long enough to drop the lawmen on a handy beach.

The "New World" was two hundred and twenty-five feet long, propelled by side-wheels operated by a powerful walking beam engine. She could reel off twenty knots and needed all her speed to outrun a British frigate off Rio. Before she reached San Francisco, she had rounded Cape Horn and eighteen of the crew had died of yellow fever. The ship was quarantined for eight days at Valparaiso. At Panama, marshals attempted to seize the vessel again, but Captain Wakeman was aided by several hundred gold hungry passengers who paid enough fares to lift the libel and let the "New World" sail on to the Golden Gate.

For the next fourteen years she ran successfully against competition on the Sacramento River, her fine accommo-dations, excellent dining room, and great speed attracting most of the trade.

In 1864, the Oregon Steam Navigation Company purchased her, took her to the Columbia and put her on the Portland-Cascades run under command of Captain John Wolf. Business at first was so good that the high operating costs of the "New World" were ignored, but when the boom busted she was sold into service on Puget Sound. She failed there and, in 1868, she was taken again to San Francisco where the California Steam Navigation Company promptly slapped a libel on her for breach of contract. The original terms of sale stipulated the "New World" would not be used in California waters until ten years had elapsed. The matter finally was litigated, and the "New World" went back to work on the Vallejo ferry run, her days of high adventure over.

THE BOAT WITH THE LONGEST NAME

When Shaver Transportation Company purchased the steamer "Cascades" they got themselves quite a stern-wheeler. Her new owners termed her, "one of the sweetest handling boats we ever had." They could have added that she also was dependable, fast, and powerful. Indeed, one writer called her "splendid." Whatever the adjectives applied to her, the "Cascades" certainly was a longlived vessel, serving sixty-one years. Equally noteworthy was the full name of the craft: "Cascades of the Columbia." This possibly was the longest handle ever affixed to a Columbia River stern-wheeler and, naturally, it was at once shortened to the more manageable "Cascades."

The Corps of Engineers built her in

Steamer "Cascades."

"Cascades" works a tow of sacked grain through fast water at the foot of Cascade Rapids.

The second "Cascades" leaves Astoria for her upriver passenger and freight run.

1882 at Portland as a workboat for Cascade Locks, then under construction. She saw little service on this oft-delayed project and, in 1888, was put to towing rock-laden barges from Fisher's Landing to Fort Stevens for the first construction work on the Columbia River's south jetty.

At this task the "Cascades" proved her worth. Back and forth on the one hundred mile run she shuttled, easily handling five barges at a time. One was secured directly ahead of the bow. On either side of this barge, but a little abaft, were two more. The final pair were secured on either side of the "Cascades" and the whole made one easily maneuvered unit. The

A stout pair of towboats, "Henderson" and "Cascades," at Shaver moorage.

"Cascades" was equal to the assignment. In one week, she moved six thousand tons of rock from Fisher's Landing to the waiting rail cars that crept slowly along the jetty's top as it pushed out into the brawling Pacific. Altogether, the "Cascades" moved more than nine hundred thousand tons of rock, plus piling and other materials, in the early years of the jetty's construction. After 1905, when the jetty was lengthened, she hauled still more.

When the Shavers bought her in 1909 she had been towing logs for a few years for the North Pacific Lumber Company and her new owners kept her at the same work. She was rebuilt in 1912. By then the lady was getting along toward middle age and a face lifting was in order.

She handled her log towing jobs efficiently, but during the 30s these became fewer as times got harder. The Shavers were happy to charter her in 1935 to an excursion operator. For a dollar a head, sightseers were transported daily from Portland to watch the construction work at Bonneville Dam. An immediate success, the one hundred and twenty mile scenic round trip continued until the start of World War II with the stern-wheeler "Northwestern" (ex "Grahamona") and the propeller "Georgiana" (later renamed "Lake Bonneville") added to handle the crowds.

Ship construction during the war gave the "Cascades" a new lease on life. She was put to handling ships from the launching ways into outfitting berths at the two Willamette River yards. It was in this service that the sturdy old steamer ended her career in 1943, burning beyond repair as the result of an oil fire explosion while assisting a ship into the deperming station at Swan Island.

After "Pronto" was acquired by the Port of Portland for a dredge tender, she was fitted with a derrick and knees.

"Athlon," a propeller steamer pictured on builder's trials at Portland, cost four thousand, three hundred ninety-five dollars to build in 1900. During twenty-one years as a Puget Sound passenger packet, she recovered the investment scores of times over.

The speedy little propeller steamer "Cyclone" (1888) was the trans-Willamette ferry between Portland and Albina until bridges and trolleys put her out of this service.

The handsome yacht "Bay Ocean," with clipper bow and raked stacks, had stateroom accommodations for fifty. She was built in 1911 to transport passengers between Portland and Tillamook for a beach resort developer. After World War I, she passed to Crowley Launch and Tug Co., San Francisco.

"Flyer" (1891), fastest propeller steamer in the Northwest, was launched at Johnston's boat yard in Portland for Captain U. B. Scott's Columbia River and Puget Sound Navigation Co. and was placed at once on the Seattle-Tacoma run. She clipped off the twenty-eight mile route in an hour and a half, on so regular a schedule that clocks were set by her.

"Flyer" afloat.

The coast defender "Monterey," built by Union Iron Works, San Francisco, visited Portland on her maiden cruise in 1893.

Kruse and Banks' shipyard at North Bend turned out the trim wooden steam schooner "Davenport" in 1912. She is a prime example of her class, a coast-wise lumber carrier making "dog holes" on the Oregon and northern California coast for cargo for southern California boom cities.

EPILOGUE

If you should happen to be at a certain place on Upper Klamath Lake or in the neighborhood of one of the San Juan Islands on just the right day you might well be jolted into the middle of next week. For around the point or down the channel, heralded by a plume of steam will come a real live steamboat. Its slow but steady headway will disdain the scurrying, noisy outboards. Its prideful captain will cast a scornful glance at lesser mortals who bounce and buzz, will examine the pressure gauge, adjust a valve ever so slightly and nod to his firemen for another chunk of wood for the firebox.

Steamer "Indian."

You'll be witnessing the revival by a growing number of ardent mariners of the only way to travel. These dedicated souls, with a passion for machinery that goes clank, puff, chug, and wheeze (so long as it is driven by steam), may number as many as four hundred in the Pacific Northwest. No one is quite sure how many votaries there are; records are loosely kept. Some have dabbled with steam autos, locomotives, or threshing machines before becoming water-borne. Others have taken the plunge into steamboating without preliminaries.

Up north members of the Puget Sound Live Steamers club have been gathering annually for almost ten years. The more persevering skippers reach the rendezvous under their own power. For some it is more expedient to tow or trailer their craft. Their wood or coal burners can't carry enough fuel for a prolonged voyage.

On Upper Klamath Lake the resurgence is a bit younger, and organization has not yet set in. Enthusiasts, however, are coming to the surface from such communities as Ashland, Medford, Butte Falls, and Central Point.

Center of all attention when the flotilla gathers is the twenty-two foot stern-wheeler "Indian," capable of turning up a respectable dozen knots, her paddle buckets threshing mightily and her exhausts vibrating in rhythm with the rods.

Though the "Indian" is the only stern-wheeler and most all the other craft are urged forward by standard propellers, one creative builder has produced a steampowered outboard engine. It is affixed to a fifty-year-old, seventeen foot hull and her proud owner doesn't mind confessing his power plant produces something less than one horsepower. He doesn't care; it's run by steam.

Though almost a century and a quarter has passed since steam first arrived in the Northwest it is heartening to know that the pioneer tradition yet is alive. And if someday as you walk along the shore you should here the unmistakeable cadence of a steam engine and note the measured progress of the boat it drives, give a cheer for the renascence. You may rest, assured that more will follow.

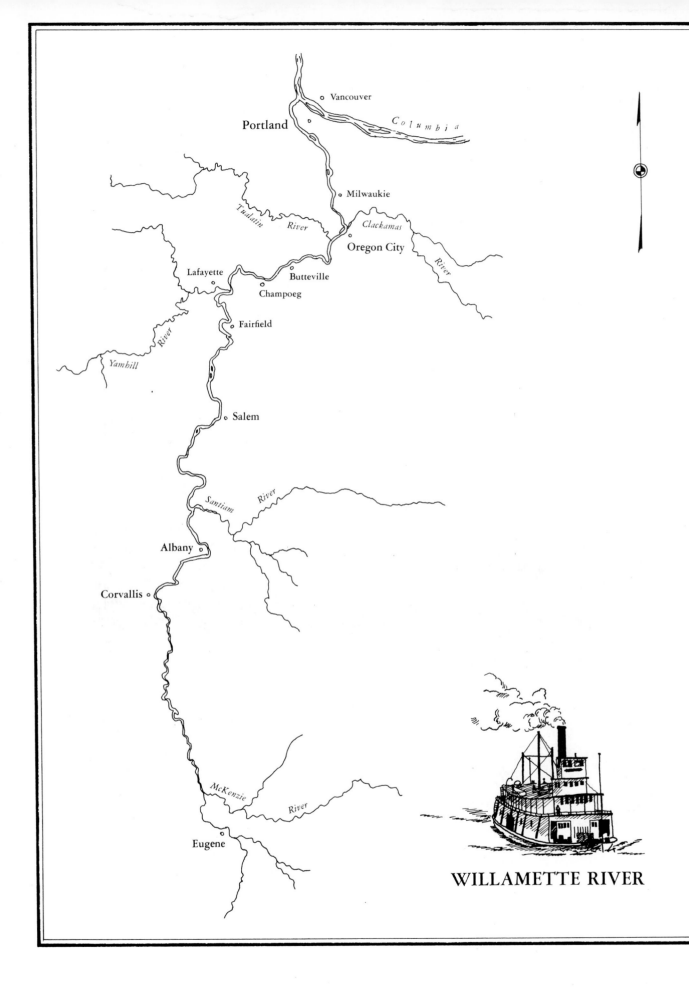

WILLAMETTE RIVER

"Ione" operated for a quarter century between Portland and the West Linn and Camas mills as one of Western Transportation Company's "paper mill fleet."

Though the Yamhill had been plied as far as Dayton by steamboats for several decades, it wasn't until 1900 that the Army Engineers built a lock at Lafayette to open up a few more miles of river. The placid, meandering stream posed few navigation problems, and after World War I, little traffic for such steamers as "Bonita."

The Oregon Development Co., a subsidiary of the Oregon Pacific Railroad Co., built "Three Sisters" and several other steamers in 1886 and 1887. The fleet operated a day service between Corvallis and Portland for several years.

With brass band blaring from the texas deck and excursionists togged out in meeting-day finery, "City of Salem" loads a capacity crowd for an 1885 outing.

For forty years, 1895 to 1935, this intriguing example of Victorian architecture stood as a lighthouse at the mouth of the Willamette River. Keeper and family occupied the four room structure, which was accessible only by boat, though it stood but a few yards offshore. After an automatic electric beacon and fog horn replaced the old oil light, the structure lay vacant for a few years. From 1946 until 1956, it served as a ship reporting station for the Portland Merchants Exchange, and a few years later vandals burned the empty old landmark to her pilings.

Nothing quite like "Uncle Sam" ever again graced the Willamette on the Corvallis-Portland run.

High iron under construction at the Wilsonville crossing of the Willamette.

Short in the hull and of shallow draft, "Ruth" was an ideal boat for the Yamhill River, which she navigated with ease between this landing at Dayton and downriver points.

In appearance, "Wallulah" was much less lovely than her name. This little gas-powered paddler jobbed on the middle Willamette during World War I.

Navigation was somewhat less hazardous after "Corvallis," an Army Engineers' snag boat, was put to work in 1877 on the Willamette and tributaries.

"Willamette Chief" was among the best of the freight boats, running regularly between Corvallis and Astoria with sacked wheat at four dollars a ton, a bargain rate that brought plenty of business. The Willamette River Transportation Co., built her in 1874, and she ran for twenty years, the last one as a lowly trans-Willamette rail car ferry.

LITTLE RIVERS — LITTLE BOATS

To the Coquille River fleet was added in 1901 the seventy-six ton "Echo" from the Ellingson yard at Coquille. J. W. McCloskey operated her for ten years. With "Liberty" and "Dispatch" (background), she puffed away at towing, passenger and freight hauling chores on the Coquille and its backwaters.

Steamboating on Oregon's coastal bays and streams developed a couple of decades behind that on more northern waters. But when they finally hit their stride, the mosquito fleets of the Umpqua, Coquille, and Coos came on with a rush. Prime reason for the lag was people, or rather the lack of them. Farmers, woodsmen, and fishermen settled in the region early. At first their isolation was nearly total. With the Pacific before and the timbered, rugged Coast Range at their backs, water or trail were the only routes to the outside.

As homesteaders staked claims along sloughs and bay shores and pushed up narrow, winding rivers toward the

Like most coast communities, Marshfield (now Coos Bay) did as much business by water as by land. Several gas launches share space with the stern-wheeler "Alert," as all wait for freight and passengers for their daily upriver runs.

forested hills, steamboat service became an absolute necessity.

The quickest and easiest way to get supplies from the settlements, produce to market, kids to school, or Mama to town for a new bolt of gingham, was by boat. Accommodating captains often saved a housewife a lot of trouble by picking up her shopping list along with the cream can on the way to town. A couple of days later on the trip up, the needles and pins, sugar and coffee, Sis's birthday present, and Dad's tobacco were dropped off with "No charge for the service, Ma'am."

About the earliest boat service was furnished by Canadian-born Captain Godfrey Seymour who started operations in 1862 on the Umpqua River with the "Raftsman." Among his later boats was the "Washington," which reached the Umpqua from Sacramento via the Willamette, the "Swan" (he was part owner and engineer on the famed Roseburg adventure), and the steamer "Enterprise."

Two Columbia River steamboat men, Captains Nat H. Lane, Sr., and W. H. Troup, established a boat service in 1873 at Marshfield (as Coos Bay then was called). Troup first had seen the bay as engineer on the "Washington" and had been so taken that he persuaded Nat Lane to return with him. Together they built and operated the "Messenger" under the flag of the Coos Bay and Coquille Transportation Company.

"Liberty" was somewhat of a wanderer. She was built at Bandon in 1903 and operated during her early years on the Coquille River. About 1907 the Smith-Powers Logging Co. brought her around to Coos Bay. Still later, she ran on San Francisco Bay until condemned and abandoned to decay on the Oakland mud flats in 1920.

Isthmus Slough, a sluggish arm of Coos Bay, meanders to a low divide that separates it from Beaver Slough, a similar extension of the Coquille River reaching northward. Though a connecting canal was infeasible, a portage railway was not. So it came about that a mule-powered train was installed in 1869 to bridge the two mile distance and a comfortable steamboat trip supplanted the tedious foot trail that connected the Coos Bay and Coquille settlements.

In 1874 a steam railroad replaced the mule line. This sufficed until the 1890s when the Coos Bay, Roseburg and Eastern Railroad made the connection complete which ended the portage.

Further north resorts were developing on Yaquina Bay under the stimulus of the Oregon Pacific Railroad. Tourist-laden steamers from San Francisco and

A couple of years after she was launched in 1914, the steamer "Telegraph" was lengthened from one hundred three to one hundred fifteen feet, which did nothing to enhance her appearance. The energetic Carl Herman produced "Telegraph" (which bore no relationship to the earlier Columbia River speedster) at his Prosper, Oregon, yard. The Myrtle Point Transportation Co. put her on the Coquille River opposite the rival gas propeller "Charm." Bitter rivalry erupted, ending only after "Telegraph" muscled her smaller competitor against a log boom. "Charm's" skipper had to beach his boat to keep from sinking.

trains from Portland and Willamette Valley points debouched eager vacationers, most of whom needed a ride to their bayside hotels. Propeller boats, mainly, supplied the service, but a few paddlers helped out. Among these was the side-wheeler "Oneatta," launched in 1872. She ran on Yaquina Bay but briefly, transferring first to the Columbia River where she converted to stern-wheel propulsion before being sent to Humboldt Bay in 1882. Later, there were the "Rebecca C" and the "Cleveland" at Yaquina, with the 1890-built "Moonlight" serving Siuslaw Bay and its backwater channels.

The "Mud Hen" of 1878 is part of regional steamboat lore. E. W. Wright, editor of Lewis & Dryden's *Marine History of the Pacific Northwest* (undisputed authority, nugget-laden mine of information), tells it best:

"The "Mud Hen" was the appropriate name given a small stern-wheeler built by the Dunhams on the Coquille River and used on Beaver Slough, a

The handsome little "Rainbow," loaded to the guards with excursionists, rounds to for a landing. Derbies and fedoras, shirtwaists and crepe de chine — it's going to be a gala day, and this bucolic Coos River setting evokes a fondly remembered, long gone era. Though she survived only eleven years, from 1912 until 1923, "Rainbow" passed through four ownerships.

tributary of that stream. The "Mud Hen" was thirty-two feet long and six feet beam, a few inches narrower than the stream, and her route extended from the river to Toledo, a distance of five miles, the shrubbery on both sides of the stream forming a complete arch the greater part of the distance.

"Every night the beavers would build dams across the diminutive marine highway, and Captain Dunham and his nephew, Robert J. Dunham, would wade out in their gum boots to remove the obstructions.

" 'What you need are locks instead of dams,' " suggested a passenger on a trip when the tide had ebbed and left a very light depth of water in the slough.

" 'Don't mention it,' retorted Lord Bennett, who was a frequent traveler on the line, 'there are locks of my hair on every crab-apple tree between the Coquille and Toledo.' "

"The 'Mud Hen' was not a thing of beauty, but she cleared her owners an average of fifteen dollars per day and was a great convenience to residents in that locality."

And that, after all, was what it was all about. The boats *were* a convenience; more, they were a necessity. Essentially, those living on the coastal bays and inlets were water people. They built their boats to tow logs to the mills that provided a livelihood for many; to carry passengers and freight and the news of the day to isolated settlements and farmsteads; for some, they forged a link with a world that often was too arduous to reach by trail or rutted road.

So the mosquito fleet grew and prospered, and it's yet at work today. Oh, the paddle boats are long gone. Gas and diesel are cheaper than steam, and faster, too. The steamboats survived longer on the Coos and Coquille than almost any place else, running well into the 1930s. But there are some around who would rather sacrifice speed for a trip on the "Echo" or the "Rainbow" with picnic basket packed, the youngsters wriggling in anticipation, and a cool, grassy meadow waiting just around the bend.

It was a short life but a busy one for "Welcome" on the Coquille River. Built in 1900 at Coquille, Oregon, the little paddler ran only for seven years before breaking her lines during high water and drifting into some trees, which battered her beyond redemption.

The busy Herman Brothers shipyard at Randolph on the Coquille produced the forty-seven ton "Dora" for the mosquito fleet in 1910. She was operated first by W. R. Panter and later by the Myrtle Point Transportation Co. until retired in 1927.

"Echo" at work on the Coquille River.

"Dispatch" replaced the smaller "Despatch" in 1903. Her owners, during the twenty-four years she served the Coquille-Bandon route, were the Coquille River Steamboat Co., Farmers Transportation Co., and Coquille River Transportation Co. From 1920, under the latter's houseflag, until she was abandoned in 1927, she ran as "John Widdi."

ROSEBURG OR BUST

Head of Umpqua River navigation was Scottsburg, about fifteen miles upriver from the South Beach terminus of the line from Coos Bay. At Scottsburg, the "Eva" met the trans-Coast Range stage from Drain, providing the connecting river link between Coast and Willamette Valley points. The Portland-built "Eva" was owned originally by the Umpqua Steam Navigation Company and later by W. F. Jewett. She served between 1894 and 1910.

At one time, practically any creek in the Pacific Northwest that could produce enough water to float a scantling was pronounced navigable and some skipper was sure to come along and try to push a steamboat up it. Once in a while the motives were questionable. As in the case of the "Swan". . . .

In 1870, at Gardiner, near the mouth of the Umpqua River, was formed the Umpqua Steam Navigation Company which built the steamer "Swan" and announced service to Roseburg. The Umpqua was safely navigable for about twenty-nine miles to Scottsburg, but there the river narrowed and the rocks came pretty close to the surface. Promoters of the enterprise figured that if a steamboat reached Roseburg even once, Congress could be persuaded navigation was practical and would appropriate funds for channel improvements.

A short distance above Scottsburg the "Swan" smashed her rudders on some rocks and tied up for a day for repairs. On she struggled another twenty-two miles to Mill's Ferry, where boiler trouble and low water put a temporary halt to the venture. She turned around and went back to Gardiner to wait three weeks for more favorable conditions.

On the second try she fared better, only knocking off the capstan and one rudder on the way to Roseburg. She reached there eleven days after leaving Gardiner, having covered the eighty-five or so miles in only about twice the time it would have taken a loaded freight wagon.

Her progress was marked by enthusiastic farmers, who foresaw prosperity when the federal government's purse would at last open and pour money into improvements of the river channel. They willingly hitched their horses to the "Swan" to help her over the high spots. They swept out a barn and danced all night in celebration at one stop. At Roseburg the townsfolk carried Captain Hiram Doncaster and crew to the nearest saloon and liberally toasted the accomplishment.

As soon as the "Swan" got safely back to Gardiner her owners published a freight tariff to Roseburg and Congress, convinced, appropriated seventy thousand dollars for channel clearance. The money added quite a bit to the prosperity of the Umpqua Valley, but neither the "Swan," nor any other boat, ever again attempted to run above Scottsburg.

The "Coos," like the "Swan," plied shallow Oregon coast streams providing the most comfortable if not the most glamorous transportation connections.

"Eva" at Scottsburg, Oregon.

When originally launched in 1890, "Alert" was sixty-nine feet long. Twelve feet were added to her mid-section in 1902, with the net advantages of larger quarters for the pilot and additional passenger and freight spaces for her daily round trip between Marshfield, North Bend, and Allegany. Sold in 1919 and transferred to San Francisco Bay, "Alert's" career there was short; a few months after arriving, she foundered, with no loss of life, near Rio Vista.

Many Coos Bay steamboatmen served their apprenticeship on the appropriately named "Little Annie," an 1876 product of William E. Rackliff, who built her at Myrtle Point for the Coquille River Trade. The diminutive trading boat survived until she fatally snagged near Bandon in 1890.

"Millicoma" was in almost all ways a typical jobbing boat. Every farmer's landing on the Coos and Millicoma rivers knew her, and those on a few sloughs besides. A dozen sacks of oats, a keg of nails and some shingles for a new barn, guards lined with five and ten gallon milk cans, "Millicoma" plodded away at her regular schedule for twenty years after her launching at Marshfield in 1909. But in one distinct respect she differed from her sisters in the mosquito fleet. When Frank Lowe built her, "Millicoma" was a steam stern-wheeler. Before long she had lost her tall black stack and imposing pilot house to become a squatty gas-powered paddler. The final decline occurred when her stern-wheel was replaced by a propeller, and she truly joined the ranks of the "stink pots."

The compact little "Montesano," eighty feet long and eighteen feet wide, was launched at Astoria in 1882 for the Shoalwater Bay Transportation Co. Her owners put her briefly in the Chehalis River trade, transferred her back to the lower Columbia between 1886 and 1889, ran her once more on Gray's Harbor, then sold her to Captain H. W. Dunham, who jobbed her on Yaquina Bay for a while. Captain Dunham later brought "Montesano" around to Coos Bay, where she towed logs for the Southern Oregon Company mill at Empire until, worn out and unfit, the old boat was laid up and stripped prior to 1900.

"Rainbow" (left) and "Alert," flags flying and steam up, lie at Coos Bay before departing on their daily round trip to Coos and Millicoma river landings.

The stern-wheel steamer "Powers" had no other destiny than to be a towboat. She was built in 1909 at the Kruse & Banks shipbuilding company yard in North Bend for the Smith-Powers Logging Co. A midships king post carried the towing cable over the wheel to the log raft astern. The "Powers'" one hundred fifty horsepower steam engine capably handled log booms in the sloughs and inlets around Coos Bay and later on the Columbia and Willamette rivers, where she worked for the U.S. Spruce Production Corporation until abandoned in 1926.

"BAILEY GATZERT," A LEADER IN HER DAY

Of all the steamboats that plowed the waters of the Pacific Northwest only one ever had a song composed in her honor. This, coupled with the fact that during her long career she possibly car- ried more passengers than any other Columbia River stern-wheeler, has caused the "Bailey Gatzert" to linger in the memory of those who were children in her heyday.

"Bailey Gatzert."

TE COLLAR LINE

Str. "BAILEY GATZERT"

DAILY ROUND TRIP—Except Monday

ncouver, Cascade Locks, St. Martin's Springs, Hood River,
White Salmon, Lyle and The Dalles

=== TIME CARD ===

Portland..............7:00 A. M.   Leave The Dalles............4:00 P. M.
The Dalles..........3:00 P. M.   Arrive Portland.............10:00 P. M.

....MEALS THE VERY BEST....

Sunday Trips a Leading Feature.
This Route has the Grandest Scenic Attractions on Earth.

LANDING FOOT OF ALDER ST.

BOTH PHONES, MAIN 351

OREGON AGENTS.   WASHINGTON AGENTS.

CRICHTON, Portland.   ETHEL McGURN, Vancouver.
HER & BARNES, Hood River.   J. C. WYATT, Vancouver
M. FILLOON, The Dalles.   WOLFORD & WYERS, White Salmon

This startling advertising notice, circa 1900, practically
reached out and grabbed prospective passengers by the
lapels.

For the "Bailey Gatzert" was a Columbia River excursion steamer and in the summer of 1905, when Portland's Lewis & Clark Exposition was drawing peak crowds, she ran twice each day to Cascade Locks, leaving at eight-thirty in the morning and five-thirty in the afternoon. She was stately and comfortable, with spacious public rooms, and the fare was one dollar and fifty cents with meals served on board.

In her honor was composed the "Bailey Gatzert March," the cover of the song sheet gaudy with a stirring picture of the flag-bedecked stern-wheeler bravely breasting the Columbia's whitecaps.

The "Bailey Gatzert" was fast, too. She made one run from The Dalles to Portland in a few minutes more than five hours — one hundred and fifteen miles of uncertain channel. And in Puget Sound, where she was built and ran for a year before going to the Columbia, she outran the swift

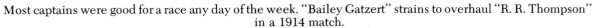

Most captains were good for a race any day of the week. "Bailey Gatzert" strains to overhaul "R. R. Thompson" in a 1914 match.

"Greyhound," only to lose the broom to the "T. J. Potter" when an exhaust nozzle blew out.

When she was launched in 1891 she was complete to the last detail, ready for her trial run. Shortly, the "Bailey Gatzert" was purchased by Captain U. B. Scott who placed her on the Columbia River in 1892 for his White Collar Line.

In 1907 she was rebuilt with a heavier, longer hull, and given engines formerly in the steamer "Telephone." Ten years later she was back on Puget Sound on the Seattle-Bremerton run. Not long after she was sponsoned out,

and fitted with an automobile elevator to emerge as the first ferry to serve the Olympic Peninsula. Her master during this phase was Captain Harry Anderson, later operating manager of the Washington State Ferry System.

The "Bailey Gatzert" was laid up in 1926, stripped of machinery and reduced to a floating machine shop in Lake Union. Aside from the memories all that remain of this fine, fast sternwheeler are her throaty whistle and ornate nameboard, preserved at the Museum of History and Industry in Seattle.

"Bailey Gatzert" makes a "mud landing" near Multnomah Falls.

"BAILEY GATZERT" — "DALLES CITY"

A festively decorated "Bailey Gatzert" beside the "Dalles City."

Back in 1915, when you could still get a bargain for a dollar, one of the best buys around was a ticket on the "Bailey Gatzert" or the "Dalles City." It bought you a hundred mile steamboat ride through some of the greatest scenery on earth. As the ad said: 'Space will not permit and words will not convey the beauty and mountainous proportions. . . ." The hyperbole was only slightly far-fetched. The advertising card of The Dalles, Portland, & Astoria Navigation Company (usually known as the "Regulator Line" after one of company's early crack boats), was detailed as to time-table and persuasive as to wonders that awaited the patron.

The "Bailey Gatzert" became the more popular of the two boats. She was bigger, faster, more finely appointed. She handled excursion crowds, making fewer stops and providing daily round trip service. The "Dalles City," doubling as a freight boat, had thirty-seven landings on her schedule, sashaying back and forth across the river to touch every town, evey hamlet.

The last great revival of steamboat travel on the middle Columbia ended with transfer of "Dalles City" into towboat service and removal of the "Bailey" to Puget Sound. But the era ended on a high note and many a senior citizen yet fondly remembers his knickerbocker days and how it was to ride the grand floating palace that was the "Bailey Gatzert."

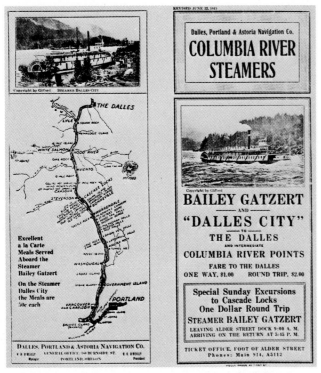

Advertising posters for "Bailey Gatzert" and "Dalles City."

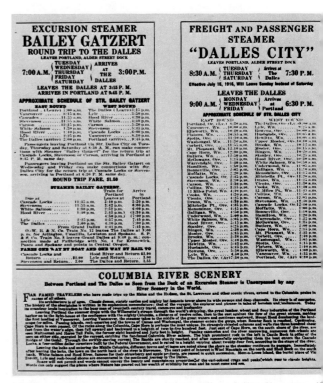

1915 schedules for "Bailey Gatzert" and "Dalles City."

Seven a.m. was traditional departure time from Portland for the steamboat fleet. "Tahoma" prepares to sail for Astoria, while "Bailey Gatzert" (center) backs around to head for The Dalles, and "Sarah Dixon" departs on her daily run to Clatskanie and downriver landings.

In 1901, photographer Benjamin A. Gifford of The Dalles snapped the "Bailey Gatzert" as she approached Cascade Locks.

Sunday excursionists, 1913 style.

"Bailey Gatzert" enters the lower lock chamber of Celilo Canal on a ten mile passage around the deadly chutes of the Columbia River.

"Bailey Gatzert" discharging her passengers at The Dalles.

"Bailey Gatzert" at Cascade Locks with a full load of passengers on August 21, 1910.

"Dalles City" at the Johnston-Olsen boatyard on Meade Street, Portland, in 1893

"Dalles City" on the Oregon side of the Columbia, opposite Wind Mountain, Washington.

"Dalles City" at the Middle Cascades.

Rooster Rock, where a state park now attracts thousands of recreationists, dominates the scenery, but not the "Dalles City," in this 1902 photograph.

THE LAST LANDING

When the time came for the Port of Portland Commission to retire its 1919 vintage steamer "Portland" from nearly three decades of ship handling almost everyone around the waterfront expected the new boat to be a propeller-driven conventional diesel tug.

Not so, said the river pilots. They expressed themselves emphatically. The Willamette channel, where it flows through Portland, is narrow and sometimes fast. In freshet time, water piles up two feet on the upstream face of bridge abutments; the current is running five knots or better. Turning a ship in the stream or threading six hundred feet of semi-helpless hull through a draw span requires maneuverability and the immediate throttle response only steam can produce.

The pilots probably didn't admit to

The wooden-hulled steamer "Portland," built as a ship-assist tug in 1919, was the first of two of that name operated by the Port of Portland Commission.

The present "Portland" with a load of passengers.

nostalgia as being a valid reason for
their choice. But a few strong votes
were cast by active old-timers who had
cut their eye teeth in a stern-wheeler's
pilot house.

So, in 1947, when the first "Portland"
was surveyed into retirement, her
replacement was ordered to be another
stern-wheeler.

By the time the new "Portland" was
launched, a goodly portion of the city's
waterfront industry had a share in her.
She was laid down at the Gunderson
Bros. shipyard by Northwest Marine
Iron Works to the design of marine
architect Guy Thayer. Final hull design
was by W. C. Nickum & Sons. The two

"Portland" chuffs her stately way along.

high-pressure single expansion steam engines were designed by Sam H. Shaver.

The pilots have been satisfied. The "Portland's" two hundred and nineteen foot length gives vital leverage when swinging ships against the current. The powerful wheel bites deeply for thrust in pushing or backing. Four main rudders and three monkey rudders, that ingenious Columbia River invention, provide maneuverability so the "Portland" literally can move sideways. When secured to a tow she becomes an integral part of that ship.

Almost best of all she is a spine-tingling sight as she sweeps through the harbor, escape valves softly chuffing, an iridescent curtain of spray soaring back from the paddle wheel, a plume of white steam spiraling from the tall black stack.

The "Portland" is a working vessel. But she has class. And, once in a while, she lets herself go as she did in the last steamboat race on the Willamette River. The occasion arose in 1952 just after the steamer "Henderson" had starred in the movie production "Bend of the River." For some time, a race between the two boats had been talked up. A three point six mile course was charted and bets were laid down.

Almost at the beginning the "Henderson" lost her steam. But her engineer put the by-pass on her and shot live steam into her low pressure cylinders to make her move. At the finish line the "Henderson's" stern-wheel was putting out thirty turns a minute, a respectable rate for a boat designed for working, not racing. The forty year old wooden-hulled "Henderson" won, and sentiment prevailed.

After that, the "Portland" resumed her quieter ways. Today she is the last commercially operated steam-driven stern-wheeler in the world. To the pilots she is a vitally needed harbor tool. To the sentimentalists she is the symbol of the past romantic era.

The Port of Portland says she will be retired with honor when that day comes to be the permanent reminder of the half a thousand steamboats that ran for a century and more on the waters of the rivers of Oregon.

The Port of Portland Commission's emblem on "Portland's" smokestack.

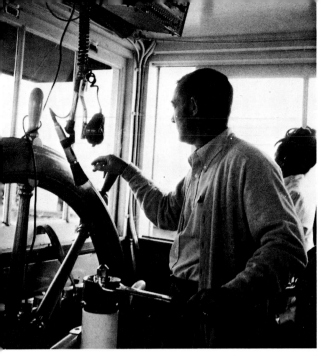

Three stories above the water, the Captain of "Portland" works his seven rudders with the aid of a steam steering throttle. The big wheel, disconnected from the steering mechanism, is dogged down, but can be freed for use if needed. Plenty of "Swedish steam," applied by two helmsmen, is needed to handle the spokes.

"Portland's" engine room is spotless as a Grade A restaurant. Two nine hundred horsepower single-expansion, non-condensing Babcock-Wilcox water-tube boilers supply the energy that drives the port and starboard pitman rods.

"Portland's" great paddle wheel.

Starboard pitman rod. The pitmans impart the entire eighteen hundred horsepower to the wheel and at the slightest pressure on the throttle the two hundred nineteen foot mass of the steamer responds as sensitively as a racehorse to the rein. That's the beauty of steam.

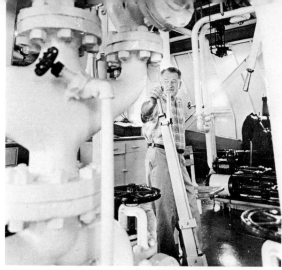

Eddie Albertson, Chief Engineer aboard the "Portland" in his "office." The engineer has been with the "Portland" for 18 years.

At the engineer's station is the steam cut-off lever, directly under the engine telegraph (left), a powered forward and reverse lever (center), and a manual forward and reverse lever (below the valve wheels) in case the power system fails.

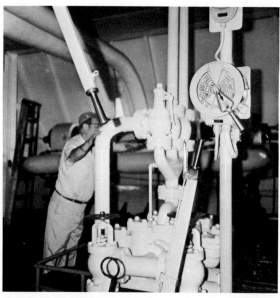

The engine telegraph automatically repeats the pilot house telegraph. Below it is the steam cut-off. The main throttle is at upper left.

The master gauge panel records steam pressure on both boilers, and feed water pressure from the two water drums is two hundred fifty pounds per square inch.

The "Portland" is a tow boat. Her port and starboard winches and tackle blocks lash her so securely to a tow that she literally becomes that ship's own rudder and motive system.

"Portland's" two water drums supply the boilers with their working pressure.

"Portland's" tackle blocks.

"Portland" assists the cruiser "Helena" into berth in Portland harbor below the Burnside Bridge, as the famed battlewagon arrives for the 1953 Rose Festival.

"Portland" assists a ship with the help of two small tugs.

"Mariposa" of the Matson Line is assisted by "Portland" and the tug "Captain George."

The first "Portland," aided by "James W," brings a newly-launched Liberty ship into the Oregon Shipyard outfitting basin in 1941.

Steamer "Portland" with a load of school teachers, an annual fall event.

"Portland" — the last working steamer on the Columbia.

APPENDIX

DISTANCE TABLES
(statute Miles)

COLUMBIA RIVER

Miles from Mouth
(outer end
of jetty)

Ilwaco	7
Astoria	14
Tongue Point	16
Altoona	24
Pillar Rock	28
Skamokawa	34
Cathlamet	40
Eagle Cliff	51
Clatskanie	54
Stella	57
Mt. Coffin	62
Rainier	67
Mouth of Cowlitz River	68
Prescott	72
Kalama	75
St. Helens	86
Warrior Rock Light	87
Morgan's Landing	100
Mouth of Willamette River	101
Vancouver	105
Crown Point	128
Multnomah Falls	136
Beacon Rock	141
Cascade Locks	144
Hood River	167
The Dalles	188
Mouth of Deschutes River	203
Biggs	207
Arlington	241
Mouth of Walla Walla River	314
Mouth of Snake River	325
Pasco/Kennewick	328
Priest Rapids	396
Vantage	425
Rock Island Rapids	453
Wenatchee	465
Chelan Falls	505
Mouth of Methow River	521
Brewster	530
Mouth of Okanogan River	533

Miles from Mouth

Bridgeport	542
Grand Coulee	590
Mouth of Spokane River	640
Little Dalles	753
Boundary	749
Castlegar	780
Lower Arrow Lake	787
Upper Arrow Lake	845
Nakusp	871
Revelstoke	937
Boat Encampment	1015
Golden	1117
Mouth of Spillimacheen River	1154
Lake Windermere	1190
Columbia Lake (Canal Flats)	1210

COWLITZ RIVER

Miles from Mouth

Monticello	2
Kelso	5
Ostrander	9
Big Sandy Bend	13
Castle Rock	17
Mouth of Toutle River	21
Olequa	26
Porter Bar	30
Cowlitz Landing	32
Toledo	35

PUGET SOUND

Miles from
Seattle

Tacoma	25
Steilacoom	38
Olympia	50
Shelton	57
Bremerton	14
Mukilteo	25
Everett	30
Anacortes	66

	Miles from Seattle
Bellingham	80
New Westminster	128
Vancouver, B.C.	129
Victoria	72
Port Townsend	40
Port Angeles	69

	Miles from Mouth
Albany	120
Corvallis	132
Kiger Island	135
Norwood Island	150
Harrisburg	163
Eugene	185

SACRAMENTO RIVER

	Miles from San Francisco
Benicia	30
Collinsville	75
Rio Vista	80
Sacramento	125
Knight's Landing	171
Colusa	250
Princeton	276
Chico	324
Tehama	373
Red Bluff	395

SNAKE RIVER

	Miles from Mouth
Perrine's Defeat Rapids	5
Ice Harbor	10
Three Island Rapids	13
Page	19
Copley's Cutoff Rapids	24
Snake River Junction	26
Pine Tree Rapids	35
Haunted House Rapids	42
Gore's Dread Rapids	49
Ayer Junction	50
Steamboat Bend Rapids	58
OWR&N Bridge/Lyons Ferry	59
Palouse Rapids	60
Riparia	67
Little Goose Rapids	72
Central Ferry	83
Penawawa	91
Pine Tree Island	101
Almota	103
Almota Dead March Rapids	105
Offield's Bar	108
Wawawai	111
Granite Point Rapids	115
Judkin's Tramway	122
Little Pine Tree Rapids	126
Steptoe Canyon	128
Mouth of Alpowa Creek	130
Mouth of Clearwater River	139
Lewiston	140
Slaughter House Rapids	142
Asotin	146
Upper Buffalo Rapids	160
Mouth of Grand Ronde River	169

WILLAMETTE RIVER

	Miles from Mouth
Portland (Steel Bridge)	12
Milwaukie	19
Mouth of Clackamas River	25
Oregon City (Willamette Falls)	27
Canemah	28
Mouth of Tualatin River	29
Butteville	42
Champoeg	46
Mouth of Yamhill River	55
Carey Bend	58
Tompkins Bar	69
Darrow Chute	80
Salem	85
Gray Eagle Bar	89
Independence	96
Mouth of Santiam River	108
Black Dog Bar	112

INDEX